*Insightful Stories & Provocative Questions that Unlock
the Hidden Secrets to Winning Big in Business and Life*

THE
SECRETS
LEADERS KEEP

BY

AmyK Hutchens

emerge
publishing

TULSA, OKLAHOMA

20 19 18 17   3 4 5 6 7 8 9

THE SECRETS LEADERS KEEP — Insightful Stories & Provocative Questions that Unlock the Hidden Secrets to Winning Big in Business and Life

© 2015 AmyK Hutchens

emerge
publishing
TULSA, OKLAHOMA

Published by:
Emerge Publishing, LLC
9521B Riverside Parkway, Suite 243
Tulsa, Oklahoma 74137
Phone: 888.407.4447
www.EmergePublishing.com

Cover Design: Christian Ophus | Emerge Publishing, LLC
Interior Design: Anita Stumbo

Library of Congress Cataloging-in-Publication Data

BISAC Category: BUS071000 BUSINESS & ECONOMICS / Leadership

ISBN: 978-1-943127-11-5 Hardcover
ISBN: 978-1-943127-12-2 Digital

WHAT PEOPLE ARE SAYING

"AmyK's Secrets *is a tremendously engaging read! By using creative storytelling followed by provocative questions, AmyK reveals the fears and foibles we all face, sparking readers to reflect on our own leadership challenges! AmyK's characters give us plenty to think about along the humbling journey to becoming a leader worthy of our followers."*

–Marshall Goldsmith, author of the New York Times and Wall Street Journal best seller *Triggers*

"AmyK is a brilliant business strategist who helped me become a better leader and a better person. Her unique blend of intelligence, insight, irreverence and practical tools skyrocketed my leadership results. As each of us prosper, fumble and reflect on our quests to become better leaders, AmyK's unique ability to always make us ask "the better question" amazes me. Her ability to intensify the secrets in each of these characters leaves you thinking, That's my former business partner, competitor, mentor or heck, this one is me!"

–David Robinson, CEO, DSM, Serial Entrepreneur who couldn't put a title on his business card until age 30

"I was thrilled to see AmyK's energy and inspiration jump off the first page of the book. I burst out laughing during the very first paragraph about Derek, the serial entrepreneur. She nailed it! AmyK has never pulled any punches and she isn't going to start now. She sees right through our personas and knows what makes us tick, what makes us thrive and what holds us back. AmyK is a brilliant educator who has taught our leadership team to define our values, leverage our talents and execute on our vision for the company. In Secrets *she reveals her insight into leaders like us—our vulnerabilities, insecurities and strengths—then shares her questions that challenge us to become the best version of ourselves. It helps me see how AmyK understands us, the real life leaders that she coaches, and sees us for who we really are—embracing our vulnerabilities as much as she embraces our talent. I am thrilled to have this new source of AmyK's brilliance and humor at my fingertips."*

–Ali Flint, Chief Financial Officer, interRel Consulting

"AmyK captures brilliant, colorful, 3-D snap-shots of leaders' complex business and personal lives. She shines such a creative, bright light on our fumbling human attempts to attain self-actualization, that I was hooked from the first story. Secrets *is a fun, insightful way to learn about ourselves, and a must read for leaders!"*

–Eric Greenwald , President & Chief Operating Officer, Grimaldi's Pizzeria

"Leadership is all about people ... starting with you ... imperfect you! The better you understand yourself, the more effective a leader you become. Secrets exposes leaders and their beliefs in this delightfully easy read. Whether you are new to the leadership game or are a seasoned veteran, your beliefs define who you are. Through extraordinarily ordinary people AmyK highlights a myriad of beliefs and consequences you will encounter in yourself and others throughout your career and then challenges you to understand, shape, and use your beliefs to effectively lead others."

–HK Bain, Chief Executive Officer, Digitech Systems, Inc.

"AmyK speaks with brilliance and authenticity. We learn our very first lessons through stories, fables and parables, and this pattern continues throughout life as we are drawn to storytellers whether in books, movies or speakers. AmyK expertly brings this renowned skill to her book, The Secrets Leaders Keep, *and this book shines with creativity. As you read her insights into the inner thoughts of leaders, may your life be enriched to the degree and capacity that mine was while reading this book!"*

–Christine Martin, author of *Recharged, Eight Ways to Lift Your Spirit*

"AmyK's creative ability to ignite meaningful reflection in our own leadership journey is a unique and valuable gift to leaders. The power in these stories is that each character contains a nugget or concept that could have been taken from my own personal and professional journey. I highly recommend this book if you are trying to improve your leadership skills."

–Paul Noris, Chairman, CEO & President, Bank of Central Florida

"You can only view yourself through a reflection or through a lens, and self-awareness requires that you look. In her new book, The Secrets Leaders Keep, *AmyK masterfully pulls us into the secret misgivings, regrets and insights of industry leaders, and in doing this, she holds up a mirror to our own thoughts, rationales and inner demons. The reflection expressively and clearly teaches us about ourselves."*

–Dr. Dave Martin, America's #1 Christian Success Coach and author of *Another Shot*

"AmyK uses storytelling to pull back the curtain, providing insights into a variety of leaders' uncertainties, fears and limiting perceptions in a most entertaining way. Her interesting and frank profiles reveal the hidden insecurities that we now know many leaders share. The Secrets Leaders Keep *is a must-read for anyone in, or aspiring to be in, a leadership role."*

–Vicky Carlson, President & CEO, LEAD San Diego

"At some point in our careers each of us has stumbled, had to face our fears, get a reality check or rethink our entire leadership strategy. AmyK lets us know that we are not alone. In fact, these trip ups and course corrections are healthy and normal! The Secrets Leaders Keep *is a must read for anyone looking to reshape their leadership paradigm."*

–Dr. Brian Carroll, Executive Vice President, Southeastern University

"*In* The Secrets Leaders Keep *AmyK proves why she is a highly recognized and respected voice in this industry. With keen insights, and her finger on the pulse of leaders' real personal challenges, AmyK provides hilarious, provocative stories and follow-up questions for anyone who wants a fresh perspective and approach to solving their own leadership hang-ups. We might think we know who we are at work and as leaders, but we all need someone to show us where we get tripped up! I mean, who doesn't want to get a kick in the pants when it actually works?! AmyK, thank you for making the sometimes painful act of self-reflection a lot more bearable, productive and fun.*"

–Katie Goodman, Comedian, Creator of Broad Comedy and author of *Improvisation for the Spirit*

to my parents,
who have graced my life
with their generous hearts

my love for them is no secret

"The purpose
of a storyteller
is not to tell you
how to think,
but to give you
questions
to think upon."

—C.S. LEWIS

ACKNOWLEDGEMENTS

GIVING BIRTH TO A BOOK is similar to having a baby, only without the epidural.

What reduced the angst and pain of this book-birthing process were those who rallied around me because they believed in me, and the message I'm delivering. Without friends and family, there would be no *Secrets* to celebrate and so I sincerely and specifically thank several of my most prominent "midwives."

I can always count on the friendship of a woman I met in Shanghai in the 1990s. We've been through a lot together. And her loyalty, support, encouragement and kicks-in-the-derriere over the years (especially with this book) underscore what it means to have someone in your corner. No matter where in the world she resides, Shary is certainly a BFF, for which I am enormously grateful and thankful.

On numerous occasions over Thai food, my dear friend, The Reverend Martha, and I discussed the choices humans make, the choices we resist and the quirkiness of life. Her theological perspective and discerning editorial eye cleaned up the characters' grammar and their life lessons. Sharing curry is apparently the perfect accompaniment to an editor's pen.

There is always the cast of characters that are so absurd, so hilarious, so real, that they turn pain into tears of laughter. The dynamic duo, Katie and Soren, are not only incredibly talented writers and performers ... they are incredible friends and cheerleaders.

Having a "test" reader who graciously read each successive draft without complaint, and who always provided constructive feedback was a blessing indeed. Mandy was the consummate "focus group" for ensuring the character's stories were easy to "follow."

Dr. Dave and Christine Martin believed in my ability to play bigger and bolder, and their support, referrals, inclusion and acceptance of me has given me a much bigger stage on which to share my gifts with the world. I'm humbled and honored that they have included me on *their* stage.

The timing of the writing of this book coincided with one of the most difficult personal years of my life. This book would not have come to fruition without the love and friendship of those who kept encouraging me to step forward. Kelley and Josh, Renee and Ben, Shelley and David, Vicky and Steve, Gayle and Fletch, Cindy and my two sister-in-laws, Heather and Karen, I'm blessed by your presence in my life.

I am the youngest of three children with two protective, older brothers. Their phone calls—filled with their kid's antics, life's projects, good-natured ribbing, unrepeatable jokes and tremendous brotherly love—are exactly what a "little sister" needs.

Not everyone gets to say their parents are truly amazing. I am one of the lucky ones. From philosophical and theological discussions to the removal of commas; from better word choices to quote suggestions; and from constructive debate to words of encouragement, not only were they my biggest supporters, they were my best sounding board. I cannot fully express my level of gratitude for their love. Bonus: they often served me wine and dinner with these discussions too.

The final phase of the book process generates a whirlwind of activities. I want to express heartfelt gratitude for Christian's belief in this vision and his publishing expertise, and Anita for her editing and book design.

Last, but certainly not least, are the numerous leaders over the years who shared their stories with me. By revealing their secrets they have given a gift to all of us—knowing we are not alone.

◄ ▲ ►

CONTENTS

INTRODUCTION

THEY STARED AT ME. Faces blank, unsure. What I was asking was strange, unsettling, too intimate.

...

Not long ago I flew to Northern Ireland to facilitate a CEO Think Tank. Located 30-minutes north of Belfast is the Galgorm Hotel, situated on 163 lush acres with it's own fishing stream, a family of blue herons and Guinness on tap. A bucolic environment for 18 all-male leaders to explore their leadership style and expand their capacity to play bigger and bolder.

I started the day's opening session with a question.

"Who are you?" I asked.

I paused for a second before adding, "Take one minute each to share your answer with your partner."

As I walked around the room I could hear snippets of their responses. These leaders described themselves as: *Father, son, husband, boyfriend, uncle, friend, brother, boss.* Over and over, they each repeated many of the same labels.

"Let's challenge you a little more," I continued. "We're going to wake your brain up. I'm going to pose another question, and you cannot repeat anything you said from your previous answer. *All new responses,*" I emphasized. "One minute each. Ready?" Heads nodded, coffee was sipped. I asked, "Who are you?"

They blinked.

"Huh?" one grunted.

"That's not a new question," said another.

"It's a new question if you can't repeat your prior answer," I replied. "Come on guys. How about, *'I like to cook. I love football and my wife,'* not necessarily in that order," I teased.

"Actually, that would be true for John," one joked, and they all laughed. As soon as the laughter died down there was a moment of awkward silence. But then they found phrases and short descriptors to better personalize their responses. *I coach my son's soccer team. I do like to cook, but only if it involves meat. I'm a vegan, but I'll eat fish. My wife is my best friend. I go to church. I raise money for kids with cancer.* Each of their minutes went by quickly.

"That was great," I sincerely praised. "How many of you learned something about your partner that you didn't know?" Heads nodded. A few eyebrows arched as if to say, *Yeah, that was not a bad exercise.*

"One more question, before we move on," I said, the energy in my voice rising. "I'm going to pose one last question, and you cannot repeat anything you said for the prior two questions. *All new responses,*" I emphasized again, "and you each get two minutes for this round." Pause. "Who are you?"

No one balked. No one rolled their eyes. They *got* it. The room was momentarily filled with silence, but it was no longer awkward. It was a silence filled with the hum of focused thinking, a harnessed energy that was palpable, and then each leader started to tell his story.

...

People have been telling stories for thousands of years. Storytelling is ingrained in our DNA. There are some aspects of life where we need to hear stories in order to better understand the message.

The 14 stories in this book reveal secrets that most leaders would not normally share—secrets about their politics, philosophies and perceptions. Secrets about who they are, how they play, why they lead in a certain way, and secrets about what prevents them from leading more effectively.

Each story is a creative amalgamation from my work with leaders. Each story represents the themes and patterns I witnessed while working with numerous executives from hundreds of companies around the globe over the past 20 years.

While each of these characters presents their own unique story, they harbor many of the same secrets and endure many of the same uncertainties and fears faced by a wide variety of individuals in leadership roles. Leaders often keep secrets because they believe others will find it difficult to understand the basis for their leadership success or failure. They believe others will scoff at the simplicity or complexity of their leadership style or criticize their work ethic. Many leaders find it even harder to share their secret fears, weaknesses and self-doubts for fear of being judged harshly or being perceived as unworthy of their leadership position.

Underneath the title, the role, or the business jacket of a leader, is a human being struggling to figure it out—a leader with secrets. If you relate to one of these leaders' struggles, triumphs or perspective, or even think, *Hey, this is eerily me*, that's the point.

Each story poses questions that as leaders we must

ask and answer for ourselves. It is only when we have answered these questions and gained insight and clarity, that our learning can be applied with wisdom. In some instances, the leader that drives us the craziest or that we find the most exasperating, is offering us a rare opportunity to reflect upon our triggers and values. Additionally, even a leader that annoys us can help us better understand the parts of ourselves we are less comfortable with accepting. Many experts say that we often dislike traits in others that we secretly dislike about ourselves. Understanding this possibility requires a bit of self-reflection and empathy. In today's increasingly complex, ever-shifting world, we need more wise and compassionate leaders willing to articulate and follow their values. And as both leaders and followers, we need to understand that leadership is an enormous learning curve for maximizing and actualizing our potential to serve.

Here's to facing your truths, answering the question *Who are you?*, finding the secrets you are hiding from others and from yourself, and realizing you're not alone in the journey of figuring out how to be a leader worthy of your followers.

◄ ▲ ►

"What, you too?
I thought I was
the only one."

−C.S. LEWIS

DEREK

Fakin' It

WHAT DO YOU CALL a highly irritable, slightly depressed, non-stop-talker whose self-grandiosity is only challenged by his own self-doubt, and who only needs a few hours of sleep a night but lots of sex? A person diagnosed with bi-polar depression. Or an entrepreneur. I prefer the label *Start-Up King*. Sold four companies for $50-million plus by the time I was 26.

I have a love-hate relationship with success. I want it. I'm good at getting it. I'm even better at losing it.

A lot of the guys I meet have competency addicton. They are so caught up in the amazingness of themselves, their inherent talent and skill, that they lose sight of the fact that they are slipping, they are on the downward spiral. Maybe it's a blessing, their addiction. They don't know they've got it: *ignorant arrogance.*

My addiction? I'm aware of it every day. The highs are high, the lows are low, and in-between is that awful sensation in your stomach that you know you've done something horrible. You're just waiting to be caught. It's that pre-break-up or post-stupid-comment feeling that makes you wish time moved a lot faster and that you weren't such an idiot after all.

That's one thing that always gets me about the whole concept of failure. We're quick to say we're all on a journey, we all make mistakes, we all mess up, but you know what? What we really mean is: You just can't do it and stay in my world, on my path, as a part of my journey. So move along. Yeah, it's okay to mess up—as long as it's before your time with me.

I was diagnosed with ADHD when I was in middle school. It was becoming a fad in some ways, but in my case it really was hard to focus. Prescribed drugs worked. Mentally I could tune in a little longer, but my personality tuned out. I got through history and math, but I'm still catching up on my own psychology. It took me six years to get my college degree. I majored in business, then political science, then econ, and finally back to business. My dad is just glad I finished. My mom said that ending up where I started—business—validates my instincts. Moms are great that way. My parents are super cool. Super supportive. I tested them over the years … too much. They and my sister Bitz are the only people who still welcomed me on their path when I failed. I'd say they don't have a choice, but actually they do. I met kids in college who had horrific relationships with their parents and I realized I was lucky. Really lucky.

My first business at 19 was diapers. Crazy, I know, but my older sister Bitz had twins. She was literally up to her elbows in doo-doo when she had a sleep-deprived burst of rage over running out of diapers one day. She wanted to know why a stupid stork couldn't deliver them to her door. I started an online diaper business two weeks later and sold it three days before my 21st birthday. I celebrated early. I was a millionaire. I made more money before I was 21 than my dad made in his whole entire life. I liked the taste of it. I wanted more.

My second business was kilts. Don't ask. It flopped. My mom expressed pure displeasure at business number three. Condoms. All colors. All sizes. Sold it after only nine months. I personally love the irony of that timing. Bitz celebrated the sale by throwing me a party with balloons made out of my extra-large product. Maybe I should have kept this biz though. The gal that bought it from me built an empire. As I said, I'm good at losing stuff too. If I'd kept it—I probably would have eventually run it into the ground.

I joined an entrepreneur organization earlier this year that pulls business owners together to help each other out, and then we go for drinks afterwards. I'm hoping that they don't kick me out. I have no business being in the room. These guys are freaking smart. It's insane. They're millionaires. Multiple times over. They made their money the hard way, unlike me. They earned it. I think a few of them might be exaggerating the money success, but they have unbelievable amounts of confidence and they get it. They know how it works. They either sold to the big players or they got to lead large organizations pre or post acquisition. They are intimately familiar with how business gets done. They know how to build and *sustain* success. They're way ahead of me. I'm not in their league.

Sometimes I can go in, order a scotch and talk their stupid ears off. Other nights it's like my throat closes, and all I can do is nod or laugh at somebody's joke. Some nights I absorb like a sponge. I'm in over my head. These people know more, they've done more, seen more, read more, traveled more. I have this dream where I'm sitting at a conference table and two cops show up to escort me out, and all the other members are snickering, rolling their eyes, and nodding like they knew I was a phony all along.

I got my MBA from Arizona State. It was less torturous than I thought because I did it most of it online. I could make sure diapers were going out the door, my fantasy football team was winning, and my paper was turned in—all at the same time. It still took longer than most, but hey, my diploma hangs on my wall like I could offer you a consultation on your kidney failure as easily as I can tell you exactly why I am not really certified to be in this business.

I was recently engaged. Sarah. I thought she was it. I thought she thought my mood swings were quirky, but it turned out she was faking it. I don't mean—she was faking being *okay* with me. My sister Bitz asked me if I was sure she wasn't faking the horizontal mambo too. It's great to have a big sister isn't it?

She gave me my ring back. Sarah, not Bitz. I mean, I didn't buy Bitz a ring. I bought it for Sarah. Bitz said that her returning it was a testament to my character and how well I treated her. I don't know. I think Sarah was just exhausted and felt guilty pretending for so long. It's a testament to *her* character—not mine. She said that she could picture way too many manic periods and that it was not how she wanted to live or how she wanted to raise a family. I'm not a crier. I can go dark, I can go inside and get quiet, but I'm not a crier. Sarah somehow found that switch. She flipped it on her way out the door.

Last Tuesday was this weird day where everything that came out of my mouth was wrong. It was like my brain was showing off just how dumb it could be. I was a guest panelist at an innovation conference in Dubai. Apparently the conference committee didn't know that I was really a fake. They were only looking at the first two businesses I had started so young and sold for insane numbers.

I won an award last year because of my new golf club design. Long story, let me just say my new clubs all but drop the ball in the hole. So there I was adding my two cents. I'd be cool with a screwy-stupid day like that except I was with strangers that I wasn't going to see again, and instead of being like, *Screw it, Derek—who cares?* It's been haunting me. It's eating at me that there are these people out in the world who only know one side of me, one slice of who I am, and it's not the best tasting slice or the most flattering side of me.

I answered the panel questions too quickly. Then someone else would speak up and his answer was better. And they were right, and it wasn't like I just had a different opinion, it was that I was factually wrong. I remember thinking, *Shut up, shut up, shut up!* But my mouth was disconnected from my mind, and it said some crazy stuff. In front of thousands of tech-savvy people I actually said at one point, "*I think the Internet is held together with duct tape.*" I'm sure they wondered if I was on drugs, because they asked me if I could be a superhero what would people call me, and I said, *The Shank-erator.* It was not good. People were confused. Was I eliminating the shanking in golf, or fostering more of it? Did I mention I'm an idiot? I could see them joking later about who got fired for inviting me to be on the panel.

I keep thinking that days like that will cause them to take away my membership cards. Right now I still belong to The Entrepreneur club, The Movers and Shakers Under Forty club, The Nice Guys Making Waves & Changing the World club, but it's just a ruse to keep 'em confused until they discover that I still need the acronym HOME to be able to say the names of all the Great Lakes. That if you asked me to name the Supreme Court justices I could tell you Ginsburg because she's Bitz's hero, or Sonia Sotomayor, which I know because the alliteration is so cool, and there's a Kennedy, but not a Kennedy from the Kennedy's, at least I don't think he's a real Kennedy, I mean he's a real Kennedy because he's alive—never mind. There's a black guy. Isn't that lame? I know there's a black guy and I can't even—Thomas! Clarence Thomas! Thank you, God. But now I'm really done.

And don't get me started on keeping track of what's going on in the Middle East. I'd blame our education system, but that's too easy. When the news comes on at night I follow it, I get it, but when it comes to keeping all these groups straight my brain is like a sieve. If you say their name, then I think, *Of course!* But if I have to recall it? Nope, ain't happening. I have to stay quiet when these things are discussed. Because the minute I'm sure I got it—I'll be a professed idiot. Ask me to overhaul the engine of your car? No sweat, I can do that. I really can, and there won't be a missing screw or a leftover head bolt. All good. Ask me who runs Canada and I'll say, "*The maple farmers and the hockey players. Pass the Canadian whiskey please.*"

Sarah was beautiful. Not Latin bombshell beautiful, more like Finland meets Ireland. She'll have cuter kids without me. But I wanted our kids. I'm having more trouble with this than

I thought. I'll be minding my own business when my brain throws down a gauntlet like, *Hey, we would have had cute kids together* or *we would have rescued dogs together. And not just little mangy ones, but big, personality laden dogs that would have walked with us, and slept at our feet, and fetched, and taken the wrap for an occasional fart that would be way too rough for me to claim.* I pictured a future. I wanted forever. Sarah didn't want manic forever. She didn't want me.

I can't sustain anything. I can't get a girl to stay with me. I don't really know how to run a business. I'm great with getting an idea off the ground. I can get it moving, but I can't keep the momentum going. I lose interest, I stop caring, or I get a new idea. In these entrepreneur meetings I act like I'm all busy getting emails on my phone, but I'm writing down the concepts or terms they use to look up later. I think if I asked what they meant out loud they'd shake their heads. I was better at asking questions a few years ago. Now I feel like I should know. I'm just waiting for somebody to find out I'm a fraud.

◂ ▾ ▸

Exploring Leaders' **Secrets**

High-performers/over-achievers often believe that they are smart, but not as smart as others believe them to be, so they worry that some day someone will discover they're at the top of the bell curve, meaning smack dab in the middle of average. These leaders, just like Derek, believe that they don't have enough intelligence, skills or talents in certain areas that warrant the position or title they hold. They worry that some day others will find out that they aren't as talented and skilled as everyone thinks they are, and they will be ousted for being an imposter.

Leaders who fear being "caught" may also avoid taking risks that could reveal their perceived inadequacies, or they settle for less, not believing they deserve better than mediocre results or average opportunities.

Fear of failure, looking foolish, not-being-worthy are fears of perfectionism, the nemesis of self-acceptance. When high-achievers move back and forth between the extremes of narcissistic over-confidence and punishing self-doubt it can prevent them from taking needed actions or cause them to self-sabotage their own efforts. Derek's feelings of inadequacies are a prime example of how our hidden belief systems about ourselves can manifest in real life mistakes or self-induced failures.

At the root of the *Imposter Syndrome* is a lack of self-acceptance. We mistakenly believe that possession of a specific domain expertise should equal mastery or perfection without a human's understandable imperfections. When leaders replace their feelings of inadequacy and paranoia about being discovered a "fraud" with realistic assessments about their valuable contributions, they focus less on their shortcomings and failures and more on how they can best use their gifts and talents to create value.

"I don't know how to act anyway,
so why am I doing this?"

–MERYL STREEP

. . .

"I still have this background
feeling that one of the
security guards might come
and throw me out."

–MICHAEL USLAN, Movie Producer

CONCEPTS

- Feeling like someone will discover we are a fraud
- Being too hard on ourselves
- Undervaluing our contribution
- Self-doubt versus self-confidence
- Feeling competent even when we don't have it all figured out

REFLECTING ON YOURS

1. When have you said or done something inane with no opportunity to correct someone's impression of you?

2. Where in your life are you "fakin' it"?

3. How might your self-doubts be inhibiting your ability to lead?

4. How might your self-talk be perpetuating your current circumstances?

5. How are you realistically measuring the value of your gifts and contributions?

"It's not your job
to like me—
it's mine."

—BYRON KATIE

HELEN

HOTELIER MOGUL

FORGIVIN' YOURSELF

UNIVERSITY PRESIDENT: ... so without further delay, I have the distinct pleasure of introducing an incredible force of nature. She is one of the top five wealthiest women as rated by *Forbes*, she was a recipient of *Time's* Woman of the Year—twice—and for over a decade, she owned the largest hotel chain in the world.

Nicknamed *The Queen of Sheets,* and one of the world's most powerful women, please help me welcome ... Mrs. Helen Norris.

Helen: Thank you. Thank you.

Distinguished Professors, Alumni, Faculty, Family, Friends and Graduates, thank you for inviting me to speak today to this illustrious institution's graduating class.

While your University President, Mr. John Williams, shared a lovely introduction—thank you, Sir—none of the accomplishments he cited give me the right to speak to you today. None of them are worthy of the request.

Rather ... it is my journey, the lessons that I learned about leadership as a child, about life as a young woman and mother, about leading myself and others as an emerging entrepreneur and ill-equipped executive that give me the right to speak to you fine, young people today ... one older leader to many young, future leaders. So I thank you, as a woman, as a mother, as a leader, as a human being, for asking me to speak about my journey today.

What do you get when you cross a roller coaster with a stopwatch?

Your life.

My mother, before she passed away, thought my life would make for a good novel. I never quite knew if she meant that it was rich with meaning or fit for a *Lifetime* movie, but I didn't ask, and I think it's good to let some questions go unanswered.

There is one question that I believe must be answered by you alone, every day, starting today: *Where are you running to?*

We can feel a lot of feelings, we can think a lot of thoughts, we can behave in all sorts of ways, but ultimately, for what gain? For what purpose? Where will this feeling, this decision lead me?

When I was growing up there was less noise, fewer distractions than you have today, but the same lessons. It might even be harder to belong today despite all this "connectivity."

When I was four, a small boy in the neighborhood dared me to eat cat food. I knew it wasn't right, but I wanted to be liked, to be seen as a brave and bold member of the pack … a conqueror of cat food. I ate two bites … straight from the dish. All of the kids laughed and called me stupid.

I ran home, tears smarting, cheeks inflamed. My mother hugged me and asked for a kiss. I refused. I couldn't. I told her I had cat breath. She kissed me on the forehead anyway. She was so good, my Mother.

When I was nine, the desire to be liked—to belong—was even stronger. There was an old elementary school up on Winslow Lane behind my first childhood house. The playground had a teeter-totter. This teeter-totter changed the course of my life. Don't look so surprised. The biggest inflection points of your life often occur with the least pageantry—and in that same up and down rhythm.

Anna and Evelyn, Cathy and Nancy … they were the popular girls, and they didn't like me. They sat at their own table, in their own clique, whispering. Too many walks home from elementary school found me feeling rejected, an ugly outcast.

Then surprisingly, one afternoon, out of nowhere, Cathy walked up to me at recess and said I could be their friend if I did as they asked. I agreed. Anything. I'd do anything. They wanted me to go hang out with Emily Draber. She was an odd one, that girl. If I befriended her they said I could join them. What did I need to do exactly? Play with her? That's it? So I did. We went on the swings, we hung on the monkey bars. I was super kind to Emily Draber and discovered she wasn't so weird after all.

Ten minutes later I returned to Anna and Evelyn, Cathy and Nancy. "Can I join you now?" I asked.

"Not yet," replied Nancy. "One more thing. Go be mean to Emily Draber. Tell her she's weird. Tell her nobody likes her. Do it and you can be our bestie forever."

I remember my heart fluttering. My gut cramping. It didn't make sense. What they wanted … it was cruel. But this was Anna and Evelyn and Cathy and Nancy. This was to be liked, to belong, to be accepted by the popular girls.

I marched over to Emily Draber sitting on that teeter-totter, and in my loudest voice I knocked her to her knees. "Emily Draber you are weird! You are dumber than dirt. I was pretending to be your friend, because I was dared. Nobody likes you!"

At first she was shocked. Not minutes earlier I had swung in the swings with her, I had laughed at her joke, I had helped her feel good about herself. She started to cry. And she couldn't stop. That poor girl. I had pierced her. Wounded her. Emily Draber and I would forever be linked by a twisted intersection of emotional scar tissue.

Nancy reported me to the teacher on duty. She said I was the cruelest girl she'd ever met. Said Emily Draber deserved better. She was right. On both counts.

Fifty-six years I have lived with that day. I don't know how others forgive themselves. How they shrug it off and say, "We were kids. Kids are cruel." I don't know how. Cathy and Nancy not liking me I can live with, not liking myself for that moment, well … failing others is painful. Failing yourself, torture.

Where was I running to? Ultimately? If I had answered that question, I would have run to Emily's friendship.

The universe repeats her lessons till you learn them. Fast forward to my first year at college. I was 18 and had finally discovered friendship. Real belonging, or so I thought. Two other girls and I became known as The Three Musketeers on campus. We did everything together before, during and after classes, and then we all went back to our separate lives at night. They were quite a bit older than me, returning to school later in life. The first of the other two Musketeers was Jennifer. She was divorced with two young daughters, but she was still living in the same house with her ex-husband. The third Musketeer was Rory. Rory was this tall, beautiful creature who didn't speak to her father. We were journalism majors. Thick as thieves until I brought it tumbling down.

It began with Jennifer's "engagement" ring. One of the largest diamonds I've ever seen, and trust me, I've seen quite a few on our hotel guests over the years. Jennifer wore it with pride. Every gesture she made featured that sparkling ring, so one day I asked her when she was getting married.

"Never," Jennifer replied, not missing a beat. "My ex-husband gave it to me. This is his *I'm sorry I cheated on you* ring. His penance."

"But you're not re-marrying him?" I asked, confused.

"It's complicated," she said, shaking her head.

I was silent. She sensed my judgment.

"He cheated," she explained. "He owes me. We live in the same house, but the house has separate entrances, our daughters have a roof over their heads, I'm going to school. I'm doing what I want. He's doing what he wants."

"And you eventually want it to work?" I asked.

"I doubt it will ever work," she said.

I was too young, too naïve, to fully understand the myriad entrances to coupledom, or the complicated nuances of how we all choose to survive. All I owned was my self-righteous sense of parochial truth. I thought she was blinded by the bling. I was on her side, believing she deserved better, but ultimately, I *was* judging her.

That was my first mistake. My second was sharing these thoughts with Rory who proceeded to go back and tell Jennifer that I thought she was only staying for the ring and the house.

The Three Musketeers disintegrated overnight. There

wasn't drama, just one phone call from Jennifer telling me I was a horrible person.

Where were we all running to?

I wonder if we had just asked ourselves this question might our answers have sent us all in different directions?

When I was 14 I craved to be 16 so I could drive. Those were the days when kids were eager to get their license. Not now. Do you think you all will be 30 by the time you decide to drive yourself? Freedom, my dear young leaders—driving was freedom.

When I turned 16, I wanted to be 18 so I could smoke. When I turned 18 I was wishing for 21 so I could drink. And when I turned 24 I wanted to stop aging. My skin was beautiful, my body was firm, I felt like I knew enough to get by. And then I blinked. I was 30. Blink—33. Blink, blink, blink, and here I am talking to you, in the shadow lands of my 60s, and looking forward to enjoying the celebratory champagne we pop shortly.

I was 25 when my first child was born. A baby girl. I was not keen on my first husband, her daddy. Okay, keen enough to conceive my Olivia, but not keen enough to stay with her daddy. It was crystal clear to me that staying with him would be a dead end for us both. I was running to better, and knew it. Later on they called these things *starter-marriages*. Back then we just called it a mess.

My second husband, Jack, Olivia's step-dad and my son Al's daddy, he's harder to decipher. He was a handsome man, really, twinkling brown eyes and a chest I loved running my hands over—don't look so shocked, I was young once. He would have given you young boys a run for your money.

When Jack, my second husband, asked for a divorce, a rug was pulled out from me. I know, I know—you've all seen so many pictures of me and Bruce in your short lifetimes that most likely you've mistakenly assumed Bruce was my only … but he's my third. And yes, he's amazing and the third time really can be the charm. I'm a lucky woman to have such a best friend now, but at the time I knew a pain, sweet children, that I had never experienced. I was in love. We were building our lives. We had so many blessings. Jack just couldn't see them. He could not stay in the present moment long enough to be happy. He was running all right, but he was running *away* from his pain, his demons. He had no clue where he was running to. Figuring that out would have required much more courage, much more strength. I was heartbroken.

Divorce was still just tiptoeing into the world. Olivia was five, my son Al two, and Al was starting to say no to everything, and that was the first word that popped out of my mouth. "No." That was what I told Jack when he asked for a divorce. No. And I can be quite forceful.

No, you cannot have a divorce. No, you cannot just leave; no you cannot reject me—us—everything we've built.

Jack could be a pain in the derriere, but he was my pain. It was not your typical, angry, can't-wait-to-get-away-from-you divorce. It was a sad unfolding, an unraveling of sorts, but I wasn't aware of this until I looked back. Really looked and saw the signs of his emotional pain. More torture. More sadness. How could I claim to be his best friend and not really see the demons of his past.

Two years later, almost to the day he initially asked for it, we divorced. Those were the years my mother stepped in. Could not have done it without her. I worked for the paper. Crazy odd hours and my mother never complained. I sold the little house we lived in. I couldn't afford to keep it. I took the children and moved into this tiny rental, a converted garage, and Olivia and Al shared a room with me. I stacked their beds, I had a thin cot, and strangely it worked. It's odd looking back. Someday you'll feel this way too. You wonder where your energy came from, how you did it, how you managed, and then you realize you might have actually had a bit of fun in there too. There are some good memories ... and consistent lessons.

Belonging is an inexplicable elixir for me. Belonging is the allure of acceptance. When I was 30 years old, my mother was a member of a book club of neighborhood ladies. One day in May, book club members decided to invite their daughters to a luncheon. My mother was the hostess, and she was a perfectly lovely hostess in her home that day. She was on a budget, what with helping us, but she took pride in her home, placing a few peonies just so, and it was always immaculate. That gene skipped me. She made little sandwiches. It was lovely. One of the book club members was a woman named Rosemary Moore. Rosemary's daughter, Naira, came too. They were part Native American Indian. Naira was as solid as the earth itself, she was much taller than I, with dark hair, these huge big eyes, and a deep, bold laugh. I liked her instantly. She and her husband had just purchased a home and she was excited. When my mother introduced us we shook hands and I was close enough to see small specks of paint on the back of Naira's hands and her cheeks. She asked me where I lived and I told her.

"Just down Smith, about a block south of the new gas station."

"I love owning my own home, don't you?" she smiled.

And before I really knew what I was doing, I smiled back and lied. "Yes."

"How long have you owned?"

"Just shy of a year."

"Who's so shy?" Naira's mother Rosemary asked, joining us with her coffee.

Naira laughed. "Helen bought her new home just shy of a year ago," she shared, before adding, "Honestly Mother you have an ear for starting rumors. I love being a homeowner don't you, Helen?"

I did. The truth was that I did love being a homeowner, only I wasn't one at that moment, and before I could say another word, my mother unwittingly corrected the lie for me.

"Oh, Naira, you must have misunderstood. Helen's just renting. Rosemary, can I touch up your coffee?"

Naira's eyes connected with mine. There was no way out.

You don't misremember whether you own or rent. You don't recall incorrectly. She was done with me before we had even started. She had the good grace to not call me on it in front of my own mother. She simply walked away.

It wasn't pretentiousness, Graduates, I wasn't trying to impress. I craved connection, something in common, to be liked and included. There I was, thirty years old and lying just to be liked. Good God—cat food, a fourth-grader, a ring, a renter … resist a lesson internally and it persists externally.

I was determined to help Olivia and Al learn these lessons faster. I withdrew, put my head down, wrote articles like crazy, started moving up the career ladder, focused on helping my children grow into kind, thoughtful, non-cat food eating beings when one night, at about age ten, Olivia brought home an invitation to join the Girl Scouts. The timing was serendipitous. We both joined. She as a Scout and I as a troop co-leader. I knew nothing about astronomy or tying ropes, had never set foot inside a tent, so I simply said I would be another set of eyes for safety. This was perfect for Ms. Mary Tufton, our no-nonsense troop leader, who ruled with an iron fist and a steadfast speed. A descendent of General Sherman's no doubt.

In some ways, I finally grew up in my thirties as the parent of a Girl Scout. I was a late bloomer, so to speak. Watching those girls on their journeys, selling cookies, earning badges, doing extraordinary things while they too struggled to figure it out. And they lied. Oh my, did they lie. To each other, to Ms. Tufton, to me, to their mothers. They called each other names, cheated for badges, ostracized a pack member when their cruel whimsies took flight. They made mistakes, made poor decisions and then they moved on … to join other groups. Perhaps these were the lessons that I was supposed to finally learn. Not that these things were right, but understanding that they are part of our humanness, part of the journey. As a leader for those girls I saw the raw desire in them to feel a part of something bigger, to belong to a group that validated them, and I also saw their unpredictable, misguided choices in their attempts to do so.

I learned two very distinct, very valuable lessons in those years. First: *We all require forgiveness*—first and foremost, from ourselves. Second: *We all need to belong.* If you want to lead brilliantly some day, help people feel like they belong to something bigger than themselves, and forgive them when they stumble in their contribution to the cause. Remind them through your leadership, your influence, your friendship, that they have worth.

Yes, I am *The Queen of Sheets*, but last year Ms. Huffington said, and I quote, "Helen Norris may be The Queen of Sheets, but it is her compassion that makes her the highest thread-count kind of Queen."

Her comment made my heart smile. We must learn to be compassionate, starting with ourselves. This journey is hard. It's not fair. You *will* stumble. And you *will* rise. Tether yourself to something or remain unmoored. Unmoored and unforgiven can be your self-imposed undoing.

It's hard to release regrets. But let go anyway. There are parts of my path I would very much like to erase, but then I wonder who I'd be today without them. If I erased all the hard parts, all the juicy parts, all the pretty stupid parts, what's left would be far less colorful, less meaningful. Less me. We don't want our downfalls to define us. But everything in life makes the equation that equals you. How can it not?

Too often we forget to include the good things we do, the accomplishments of service, the moments of pure generosity and compassion. We are complex beings, so complex, and the less judgmental I am, the more accepting, the more compassionate I am with myself and others, a better person emerges.

Leaders should not confine themselves to creating followers. Leaders must accept responsibility for creating more leaders. I learned very quickly in business that the best way to do so was to be vulnerable—to share my mistakes and missteps with others. Not only could my followers learn from my mistakes and avoid those same pitfalls, but when they had their own transgressions they knew I would safely support them as they too emerged into leaders of themselves and others.

The rest of my story you know. The last 35 years have been well documented. Today, I wanted to share the foundation underneath all those hotel rooms—the story that you didn't know. The woman *behind the sheets*.

As a journalism major turned mother, turned bed-and-breakfast owner, turned board member, turned sales executive, turned COO, turned hotelier mogul, turned grandmother;

there's only one question, dear Graduates, that you must ask and answer each and every day: *Where are you running to?*

◀ ▼ ▶

Exploring Leaders' **Secrets**

As an executive, Helen was known for her self-effacing manner, for being true to herself and for her compassionate demeanor. While she was hard on herself for her early childhood offences, she eventually used these experiences to transform the way she led herself and others. Helen reflected upon the valuable lessons of her formative years: and she refused to let a few regrettable moments cripple her potential or truncate her ability to lead a life of purpose. As a result, she benefited as a person and her followers benefited from her leadership.

Intrinsic worth begins from the inside out. Self-forgiveness, specifically, keeps us moving toward living healthier lives so that we can better serve ourselves and those we lead. Living our lives from the inside-out is directly linked to our ability to accept and respect ourselves so that we may better accept and respect others. Helen, unlike many leaders, faced her shortcomings, forgave herself, and used her early transgressions to fuel her ability to lead others with greater compassion and empathy later in life.

Self-forgiveness is a form of letting go. Letting go of past indiscretions and old resentments, letting go of yesterday's pain and today's guilt. Letting go of resentments and grudges against ourselves is perhaps more difficult than letting go of others' trespasses against us, and yet, it's imperative for leaders to do so. Leaders who practice self-compassion, without a need for restorative justice, wish themselves well and are then able to extend true compassion, understanding and forgiveness to others.

Self-compassion is not selfish. To believably give grace and offer forgiveness to others we must be able to first receive it ourselves *from* ourselves. Receiving forgiveness does not deny our responsibility nor accountability for who we are and what we do, it simply pays homage to our flawed, imperfect humanness. Self-compassion also frees us to move forward more effectively, without the trappings and weight of our transgressions so that when others experience similar circumstances, leaders show up with empathy and wisdom rather than condemnation.

Choosing to live from a state of self-doubt and self-condemnation perpetuates a selfish focus and limits leaders' ability to lead productively. The better care that leaders take of themselves, the more effective they will be for and with their followers. If they are consumed by their own shortcomings and faults, their own mistakes and limiting beliefs, they are not able to show up mentally and emotionally focused for others. Leaders must face their transgressions, accept responsibility for them, and then release these transgressions. By replacing our offences with understanding and wisdom we transform prior mistakes into wise, compassionate actions and responses further down life's path.

At its core, self-forgiveness is about diminishing our self-loathing or self-contempt in response to hurting someone else and reconciling with our selves.

When leaders ask *Are we helping or are we hurting?*, it's easier to answer this question with respect to intrapersonal situations. Prior to difficult or critical conversations, leaders can craft questions based on this exact premise. *Will this question help or will it hurt? Is there a way to phrase it or frame it that will be more helpful and less hurtful?* However, leaders also need to ask this of themselves: *Is my self-censure and criticism helping or hurting me? How might I accept responsibility for my actions, and move forward in a way that now helps others rather than hurts them?*

Self-compassionate leaders understand that our intrinsic worth is independent from our offences. All of us have a success story still to write.

"If your compassion does not
include yourself—it is incomplete."

–JACK KORNFIELD, Buddhist Monk

• • •

"Identity does not grow out
of action until it has taken
root in belonging."

–CHARLES MARTIN, Author

CONCEPTS

- Belonging
- Self-forgiveness
- Compassion and empathy for others
- Learning the lessons from our transgressions
- Being vulnerable
- Creating future leaders; not just followers

REFLECTING ON YOURS

1. How easily are you able to forgive: yourself and others?

2. How do "acceptance" and "belonging" influence your choices and actions?

3. If you were to love your followers as you love yourself, should your followers be warned?!

4. What are you resisting internally that continues to show up externally?

5. Where do you belong?

6. Where are you running to?

◄ ▲ ►

"When I discover
who I am,
I'll be free."

–RALPH ELLISON, *Invisible Man*

KYLE

LEAVIN' THE 'HOOD

MY DAD IS THE FAMOUS "Pop-Tart Preacher." Twenty-thousand people fill his stadium every Sunday like Pavlovian dogs. Only instead of Grade-A prime they get pop-tarts. Highly addictive, super-sweet goodness. I don't blame them. It's hard to deny the allure of a pop-tart. It's a guilty pleasure for some. They say they like their fruits and vegetables, but open the closet and you'll find a Costco size box of frosted strawberry rectangles tucked just behind the unopened bran flakes.

Pop-tarts aren't my thing. No offense to my dad. He's cool with me now—sorta. He was not excited when I told him I was leaving to start my own church. *Offended* was one word he used. *Betrayed* another. He minored in theatre so it was a pretty good Willie Loman meets Billy Graham routine. He offered up silence for about six months and then when I opened the doors to my new church he got his best friend, Pastor Dan, to fly in and wow everybody in his congregation while he came over to hear my message.

"Deep," he said. "Too deep for my blood."

Translation: *Can't put it on a bumper sticker.* If the message doesn't rhyme or include the word *prosperity* or *promises* he doesn't get it. I thanked him for coming. Told him that I loved him. I do love him, and having been raised by a guy that swims in the shallow end of a "light" message, it's easy for me to say those words. It's just not easy for me to live on a diet of sugared pastries, even if you spread the agave jam on them.

My dad and I are more similar physically than we are spiritually. Spiritually, it's a stretch. Physically, it's cookie cutter. We are almost identical so I thank him for being good looking, but he keeps a clean shaven face with a smile that says, "I love my God, my Mama and apple pie." I prefer my goatee, "I love my Jesus, my rebel de jour and a shot of tequila" smile.

Also, I'm more charismatically challenged than he. He oozes charm, I ooze intensity. Still, we look very much alike. When I was little and tagged along on his daytime neighborhood ministry visits, it was completely safe for him to tease the housewives about my origins. He would tell them he was out preaching on that day when the milkman delivered … *wink, wink.* It was him being funny, because I was his identical looking son. There was no denying that I was his kid. A true PK. Women would giggle at the implication of his wife's naughtiness all the while wondering just how naughty they might be should he stroll from the porch into *their* living rooms. My dad was very good looking, and he warned me when I was 16 that an offer for lemon poppy-seed muffins had brought down better preachers than he. As an adult I learned firsthand the temptation of muffins. My dad never succumbed and I too can't eat a muffin to this day—that's a literal comment—serious indigestion. A reminder of his wise fatherly counsel.

Many people want their God in a box. Neatly labeled, neatly categorized, but God is too nuanced for a single label. We had a line on our website's homepage, "God cannot be put in a box." Unfortunately, with the name *The Tombstone,* this just increased the calls for cremation services. In hindsight, we should have paid $100K for the domain name: *The Summit.*

We tried buying the name *The Rock,* but it was already taken. As was *The River, The Hill, The Knoll, The Spring, The Valley, The Unified, Tilted Saddle, Landmark, North Cavalry, South Cavalry, West Cavalry* and *The Creek. The Tombstone* was taken too, by a guy selling genuine tombstones, but Mitch, my praise band leader, offered him $15,000 in order to call our church *The Tombstone,* and the guy took it. We thought we were saving $85K. He said more people are cremating these days and he was looking to retire anyway. So here I am, the Pastor of *The Tombstone* with a huge gray slate on our roof that does double duty in October for our haunted house World Missions fundraiser. In mega-church parlance we're small but mighty—3,000 strong—who now show up on Sundays, coffee in one hand, iPhone Bible app in the other, to hear … well … a more protein-packed message.

Since I'm the Senior Pastor, a lot of people want to know if I've actually killed God. It's not as bizarre a question as you might think. *The Tombstone* name choice has been a blessing and a curse. We get lots of hate mail because people misinterpret the tombstone as that of God's. So let me be clear. It is NOT God's tombstone. God is alive and well. It's your tombstone. Now, you're a child of God, living out the gifts and talents He gave you, so technically, it is God's tombstone, but that usually freaks people out, so I just leave it at, *It's yours. What would your tombstone say about you?*

Lots of people then bring up the famous dash poem. You know, that the dash between the year you were born and the year you died is highly significant as it represents your life.

We're all then supposed to get really contemplative about our dash, and thrash around in our heads to see if we've chosen wisely in making a splash or if we've wasted it and watched it go by in a flash. Ugh.

If you want to hear that message, go to my dad's church, The Star. He delivers a great sermon on packing your dash with random acts of kindness. Frosted Cherry...so tasty!

Should there be anything less random than kindness?

Two months ago a *Rolling Stone* journalist asked, "If your dad is the Pop-Tart Preacher, who are you?

I instantly replied, "Bacon in Bed." I regret saying that to a reporter because I have suffered the cartoons, the late-nite comedians, the SNL skit, but it really was an instinctive response and it carries so much truth. But it's a terrible sound-bite and Peter, our church publicist, was having a cow trying to get a handle on the public relations before the article was published. Mitch laughed so hard he's writing a new song all about bacon so we can show the world that we can laugh at ourselves, but it really was a dorky thing to say. It's just … it's the truth. The truth always comes out … especially with bacon and beds. How often do we find ourselves at three in the morning, wrestling with our deepest, meatiest questions while strangled by our own sheets? That's what I was trying to say—if my dad is pop-tarts, I'm bacon … but in bed, in your darkest moments. My God wants to be with me during the tough times, when the demons show themselves, not just the prosperous times when all is cool.

But it sounds so wrong until I explain myself, and by the time I explain myself it's too late. People have already presumed I'm an idiot and there you have it. I am the Bacon in Bed worshiper with God's tombstone on my roof. I can see the headline now: *If Satan was served breakfast in bed, might he prefer bacon or pop-tarts?*

I'd tell you I'm a brave rebel, defying my dad and going my

own way, but I cried when my dad stopped talking to me. Jesus had to leave his neighborhood to grow into the Messiah, and I think that's a parable for us all. We cannot fulfill our potential when we stay within the confines of how our early neighbors or family members define us. Breaking out of these first roles is often harder for the neighbors than it is for us. I ran into a friend from high school the other day. He was shocked to learn that I was a preacher.

"What makes you qualified to be a preacher?" he asked, truly dumbfounded.

"Seminary," I replied out loud, followed by an internal, "Idiot savant." I was not the most popular kid in high school, and sometimes my shyness or awkward comments got perceived as being more stupid than I was, but I was just uncomfortable in relating to these other kids who always seemed to have their act together.

"How many people in your church?" he asked.

"A little over 3,000 people. Every Sunday." I will not deny my ego was stoked to hear this fact out loud. But the look on his face was disbelief, and my confidence started to yield to hurt. I was beginning to feel like an excluded freshman again.

"I never knew your brain wired fast enough to lead 3,000 people," he said, completely oblivious that his words were a slap to the face.

Yeah, I turned the other cheek. My dad may be full of slogans and clipart, but he raised me right. I smiled. Full wattage. "Isn't it great we get to grow up and leave behind the silliness of high school identities," I said. "Great to see you. God bless." And I walked back to my new 'hood.

I shouldn't let a kid from high school bother me so much. Like the Buddhist monk who mentally carried the beautiful woman on his back after his fellow traveler had set her down miles earlier, I should have mentally set him down long ago too, but I find him on my back too often these days. I can't forget his words. He only said them one time, but I replay it constantly.

My dad always said I was overly sensitive, but where's the line drawn between being molded and shaped by all of our experiences and letting go of the past? Letting go of what others' want us to become, what others want us to believe as opposed to what we have found, through our own experiences, to be true?

It's these moments of uncertainty, of self-reflection, that I find the most exhilarating and haunting. The older I get the more certain I am of honoring my core, of separating definitively from the pack that cannot grasp that I want to be something even bigger and braver than any of the neighborhood kids thought I might be. It's just not always easy. I wrestle with ambiguity and shades of hesitation to this day, hence the bacon comment.

But most of us crave certainty from our leaders, our role models. We push boundaries as kids to assure ourselves that their definitiveness is firm, but we push boundaries as adults to create new limits, new certainties, and this is good. We step into unchartered territory creating even more distance between who we are destined to be and the limitations of what others wanted us to be. Most days I find myself leading from the edge of a grounded center.

It doesn't stop. I won't sweeten the truth. There are days I identify more with doubting Thomas than I do with devoted Peter. Then there are days when I experience such clarity, such a strong sense of knowing that I'm headed toward a better self that I blurt out thoughts like *bacon in bed* because I'm certain, truly certain that in darkness we experience the brightest light, the most truthful truths. These moments are usually when I mistakenly believe that I'm wrestling with sheets and insomnia instead of my expanding soul.

◂ ▾ ▸

Exploring Leaders' **Secrets**

Just as Kyle discovered, forging a healthy, unique adult identity, and realizing our greatest gifts and talents, often requires saying goodbye to our old neighborhood, our old identity and our old labels. Changing what people from our past think about us is difficult and at times downright impossible. When we focus on changing the image we project of ourselves, rather than wasting energy and effort attempting to change others' visions of us, we can more easily and healthily live into an image that counters prior negative messaging.

Removing other people's perspectives and limiting beliefs about who we are and how we might play in the world allows us to evolve into our fullest potential.

Kyle is a classic example of someone whose credentials and training as a minister are questioned by an individual from his childhood. Many theologians have a hard time with family and friends taking them seriously later on in their careers. Theologians are not alone. This difficulty is faced by almost all leaders.

How did glue-sniffing, five-year-old Joey become a CEO?

How did cry-baby Carrie become such a hot-shot litigator?

How did pathetic Patricia acquire five patents?

It also hits closer to home. Parents, siblings and/or significant others "know" us in a certain role, and when we change this role we often meet resistance. Why? Because for our role to change, their roles must change as well. The overweight child or spouse chooses to exercise and be healthy, leaving other overweight family members or spouses to feel rejected or judged, and even the thin family member then loses his status as the only one. A son or daughter is the first to seek higher education and other family members and friends question why the education is needed, sometimes even criticizing the young adult's choice by saying, "He thinks he's better than us."

Leaders know that who we were yesterday is not who we are today nor who we will be tomorrow. Transformation is part of the human journey, and yet, even though we all understand that humans evolve, too many people wish to evolve while keeping others in a box, or some people resist change so much they try to keep everything status-quo for as long as possible. Others understand that evolving is part of the journey, they simply struggle with which aspects of themselves to preserve and carry forward and which aspects to shed along the way.

Questioning the sources of our belief-systems allows us to recognize where, how and why our stories started. Childhood bullies, critical adults, jealous friends are just a few possible primary programmers of damaging messages. What these negative naysayers might have said once, we often repeat hundreds of times until the noise becomes a deep, imbedded belief. Or perhaps they did repeat hurtful comments enough times to make it extraordinarily difficult to discern their version, their story, from a more honest reality.

On the flip side, progressive peers, loving caregivers and encouraging teachers may have been early programmers of positive beliefs that served us well as children and still apply today. Or perhaps their affirmations of our worth and talent served us well at the time, but are no longer relevant or not as nuanced as we now require. Either way, they bolstered our self-esteem and self-worth, and now we need to discern what we wish to carry forward, what we need to refine, modify or expand and what we need to leave behind.

Leadership requires that we have clarity and confidence in our core values and individual identity. Being aware of influences from our youth and taking stock of what influences our sense of self and our identity today: people, places, media outlets and more, increases the likelihood that we are projecting our best self forward and not the version others have draped upon us or confined us to for their convenience. *Leavin' the 'hood* requires sifting through our past, selecting what we want from yesterday to bring to today, and consciously choosing who we will become tomorrow so that others will want to follow our lead.

"Most people are other people.
Their thoughts are someone else's
opinions, their lives a mimicry, their
passions a quotation."

−OSCAR WILDE

. . .

"I am no bird; and no net
ensnares me: I am a free human
being with an independent will."

−CHARLOTTE BRONTË, *Jane Eyre*

CONCEPTS

- Accepting and rejecting previous sources' beliefs
- Finding truth in light and darkness
- Keeping others boxed-in
- Accepting identity evolution in others
- Choosing healthy sources to fuel current individuality
- Establishing individualism and independence
- Evolution of spiritual freedom and self-defined faith

REFLECTING ON YOURS

1. What comments, perceptions or opinions from others do you need to let go of and leave behind?

2. When have you boxed someone into a role or assigned a limiting label that impinged upon his or her evolution?

3. Who has questioned your training, credibility or knowledge for serving in a specific role? How did you respond?

4. How might others' disbelief, judgment or criticism of your expanding capacity be a reflection of their own assumptions and struggles in leaving their past behind?

5. What do you choose to believe to be true about your identity today?

6. Have you left your 'hood?

"I wanted to
be good, but I
wasn't sure if I was
prepared."

—LEILA ABOULELA, *The Translator*

PIP

CEO

BEIN' ENOUGH

WHEN TOM WINTON texted me last night to share his disbelief at being fired I called him immediately. I said all the right things. That's what best friends do. I was supportive, encouraging, snarky about his chairman—I even got him to laugh. I was a good friend on the phone if not all together a weak one. Not sure I could have pulled it off in person.

I am Tom's biggest cheerleader. I helped him climb a few rungs on the ladder in our early careers. Seven years ago when he made it to CEO before me I sincerely toasted him with champagne and cried much later that night, pumping my fists against a glass ceiling that I was apparently not strong enough to shatter. Immature? Yes. Human? Yes.

When I made CEO 14 months ago, Tom called and shared his condolences. He was a bit more cynical, more frustrated, more disillusioned. He'd always believed he'd gone into business to avoid politics, but politics are strong in business. Despite his sardonic disposition … he called, and I'm pretty sure he wasn't wishing my downfall, just wondering if it would be easier for me than him. And if it did turn out to be easier for me, I expect he would someday tease me in a bar, humorously saying "*Screw you*," all the while wondering how I got so lucky. How did I get greater results than he had gotten in the same role? It's sad when insecurity trumps friendship.

Tom and I met in the tenth grade. In 1971, my family moved from Santa Barbara to Washington, D.C., and I was in culture shock and weather shock. Who knew you needed a wool coat in April? I arrived at school in a t-shirt and skirt, goose bumps covering every millimeter of my body. Tom gave me his coat at lunch rationalizing that his hat and gloves would be sufficient. His friends teased us, but he didn't care. He shouted back, "Don't you guys have sisters?"

I stood out. Not only was I ill-dressed, I was tan and my hair uncombed. A dark, sun-kissed otter in a sea of jellyfish.

My parents knew very little about inner beltway politics but quite a bit about anti-Vietnam protests, as Reagan had sent the National Guard to our campus at UC Santa Barbara because of the bombing of the faculty club a few years prior. When protestors started burning buildings my parents applied for new teaching positions. Someplace healthier. Someplace safer. I'm not sure Washington, D.C. was exactly that more benign, healthier place, but my mother's brother, Uncle Bob, had an empty basement apartment. Free rent trumps romanticism.

D.C. teemed with labels, economic hierarchies and backroom whispering and posturing, but we eventually found our enclave of emerging hippies, despite my Uncle's disapproval. Tom's family was the opposite, and I think that's why the gravitational pull was so strong. They were formal, neat—so not us—and Tom accepted me anyway, despite his mother's disapproval. To her, I was a sick, stray dog in need of being put down. To Tom, I was an unkempt rescue with loads of potential … I just needed a good groomer.

It was Tom's father that actually encouraged our friendship. Tom had invited me to dinner the day after sharing his coat. His mother was not pleased, but she set a plate on the table for me anyway. His father arrived home from work distracted by current events and stock market shenanigans. Tom introduced me but his father did not comprehend the reality of my presence until he made an off-hand quote halfway through the meal.

"Religion is the opiate of the masses."

I raised my head and asked. "Do you like Hoffer?"

Mr. Winton's head jerked in my direction, fully acknowledging my presence for the first time. "You read Hoffer?"

I nodded. In that moment I was unaware that he was impressed with me. It was just comforting to engage in the type of dialogue I had experienced in my old living room or on campus sitting with students. If I was an unobtrusive pet, they would stroke my hair and banter back and forth and I loved being included. "Hoffer thinks hatred springs from self-contempt."

"And what do you think?" he asked.

"I think preachy self-righteousness is a mask for guilt."

"And the link from guilt to hatred?"

"Our inadequacy."

He sat back in his chair and just stared at me. I lowered my eyes, I remember heat rushing into my cheeks, burning with embarrassment. I'd obviously said something stupid and he was about to tell Tom that I had been found out for the fool I was.

"Tom, where did you discover this lovely young lady?"

I looked up. Mr. Winton's eyes were sparkling at me. Less so Mrs. Winton's.

"In the school yard, freezing to death," Tom replied, swallowing another large piece of roast without fully chewing it.

"You gallantly saved her?"

"Yes, Sir."

"My guess is she'll return the favor."

And with that, Tom was my new best friend. Still is.

We've weathered a lot together: inept bosses, fractured silos, outdated systems, entrenched bureaucracies, and the feelings of inadequacy in boardrooms—others' and our own. In fact, inadequacies are daily background noise for leaders. Most executives I worked with over the years craved being seen as powerful—not human, not vulnerable. It was easiest for them to help the guy way down the ladder while surrounding themselves with mediocre talent because mediocrity is not a threat to their worth, their value or their title. But it drove 'em crazy at the same time. They yelled at their employees, *"Why can't you be smarter, stronger, a thinker? Why can't you fix this, solve this, rework this?"* Or, they just sighed and kept these thoughts to themselves all the while perpetuating mediocrity from their throne of insecurity.

How do I know this? Because these insecurities reside within me too. The words *I don't know* lurk in my stomach, churning, roiling, creating tremendous distress, but they cannot rise—I cannot let them out. It is far easier for others to accept that as a corporate executive I do not know how to remove a spleen than it would ever be for them to accept that I am not entirely confident with numbers. I intellectually understand that my controller will help me with numbers, that the engineers will explain the designs, and that my gift is my ability to ask the insightful questions, strategically connect the dots, align the pieces, see beyond the numbers, beyond the designs, and yet, the fear of my inadequacies being discov-

THE **SECRETS** LEADERS KEEP

ered has created my own pattern of competitive, destructive behaviors. I have two main thoughts on the internal tickertape running at the bottom of my consciousness screen. *I am not good enough. I do not have enough.* These feelings started early.

Hoffer made sense to me in a world filled with cruelty and judgment and helped me to accept that Mrs. Winton's scorn was a reflection of her inner illness and not my outer dirt. But still, I wanted to be good enough anyway.

That Mr. Winton found me intellectually curious was not so helpful for my relationship with her either. Tom and I would curl up in blankets in front of the fire on cold winter nights and Mr. Winton would read from Frankl, Dahl, Conrad, Kipling and others. Mr. Winton loved thinking about and exploring ideas. He taught us to question, to debate, to look at the world through multiple lenses. Tom would humor his father for an hour, but then his brain would tire and he just wanted the story, not the story behind the story or even the alternative plot line. He just wanted to read. So I would pick up where he left off becoming all the pupils that Mr. Winton never got to teach by going into business. I was an excellent student, a natural byproduct of my professorial parents.

Mrs. Winton would come downstairs and seeing that we were still huddled in front of the fireplace, she would sigh, loudly. Mr. Winton was respectful and never made her sigh more than once, and I knew that leaving immediately would grant me another night sooner rather than later.

Those nights enhanced my understanding of people, my

intuition, my ability to express and feel empathy toward others. They did not however advance my financial acumen, for as savvy as Mr. Winton was with market fluctuations and turning a dollar into ten, he never once wanted to teach me how to do it.

"It won't bring you happiness, Pip-squeak," he'd say when I would ask him to explain a bull or a bear market. "Spend less than you make, save wisely and marry a man smarter than you. The last will be your biggest challenge." It was a compliment from a man divided by two different generations.

And so, the people side of me flourished. My somewhat irreverent view of authority helped make me a natural leader of others. That is, others were willing to follow my lead. I was willing to openly question dogmatic authority when others were too afraid. Intuitive understanding and empathy was in my DNA and reinforced by my environment. But I lack business acumen, and so the irony is I am now CEO of a Fortune 1000 company, constantly waiting to be found out. Always looking over my shoulder to see if someone might discover I am not as smart as I appear to be. Meanwhile, clue-free, over-confident leaders sail through the day oblivious to the reckless ripple effects they make impacting innocent lives. As I said, we are driven and haunted by our inadequacies.

Tom, on the other hand, had gotten a peculiar combination of his parent's genes. He was as financially bright as his father, as thoughtful in his support of the underdog, and yet, could be as cold as his mother at the oddest times. This distancing from others made him unpredictable and caused others to perceive him as untrustworthy. It was sad when he was fired but we both knew why. Tom had loyal followers, people that over the years had jumped companies to continue to serve as his beloved lieutenants, but Tom had dissenters too. Managers who knew Tom didn't much care for them, and Tom was unqualified at being reserved. He didn't have the energy for affability nor office politics.

Right after college graduation we had the most intimate conversation we would ever have regarding our friendship.

"You are the best person I know," he had shared, throwing back his third shot of celebratory tequila. I blushed. "And I won't ever kiss you."

"I didn't ask you too," I responded defiantly, secretly stung by the rejection.

"It's not because I don't want to. It's because I do." He leaned in, his nose almost touching mine. I could smell the tequila on his breath, see a piece of lime pulp on the edge of his lower lip. "One kiss will make me want more, but here's the truth, Pip-squeak. I can't marry you, and I don't want to use you or hurt you." He pulled back and motioned for the bartender to pour another shot.

I'm sure the look of confusion on my face is what prompted the longest speech Tom has ever spoken to me.

"You're it, Pip. You're the whole package. You are brilliant and beautiful and my best friend. My father adores you, my mother well … she did make you a pound cake at Christmas, a lot for her, and yes, I want you too. I want to tuck you away and have you all to myself. God, that sounds creepy, but you know what I mean. But you and I … you know me too well. I can't hide my secrets from you."

"I don't want you too," I interrupted him. "Best friends don't have secrets."

"Exactly … that's my point. I'm not as smart as you. I'm not as good with people. You know … "

I cut him off. "You're just as smart as me. You know numbers in a way that makes my head implode."

"No," he countered. "If you really cared, you'd be great at them … I can't hide my faults. I want to be with you, but I need somebody who doesn't know everything about me. I need someone who knows me just enough to know I'm human, but will wake up everyday and think I'm the man."

And once again, Mrs. Winton's DNA and Hoffer came face to face. Tom's angst was not a reflection of me. He doubted himself and he let his doubts drive his decision-making.

"I accept you just as you are," I whispered, knowing that it wasn't enough.

Tom was prey to the perception of his own inadequacies. He wasn't good enough. He didn't have enough. He had filled in the blanks with his own limiting beliefs. I nodded, understanding that no matter how much I wanted a different ending, the only person that would change his beliefs would be him. I sucked it up and croaked, "You will always be my best friend, Tom Winton." But it wasn't enough. I wasn't enough.

His father was wrong after all. I would not return the favor. I could not save Tom from himself.

He nodded. "Pip, you need a shot of tequila to wipe that look off your face."

Praise is inner health made audible. C.S. Lewis. He's right. When you are no longer bound by your inadequacies—your *"not enoughs"*—it's easier to be genuinely complimentary and supportive of others. As for Tom's quote: *I want you to be successful … just not as successful as I am.* And he means this sincerely. It's not his most endearing trait, but it's his truth. I am a witness to his competitive jealousy as well as his envy of others. His envy of me. An envy that could not translate friendship into love.

I have seen overachievers' actions say I applaud you and am happy for you, but their eyes crave your stumble, or if not your stumble then at least their advancement beyond you, over you, by you. Tom never wanted me to stumble, still doesn't, he just wants to get there first. Over me, around me, in front of me. This is the price we leaders pay when others see in us a fulfillment of their own blocked desires and needs.

Every leader has their quote. My quote? *"Every good person questions if they are enough. Every good person struggles to answer yes."*—Pip Martin

Exploring Leaders' **Secrets**

Many successful, smart, talented leaders believe they are neither *good enough* nor *have enough* to play in the coveted sandbox. They end up behaving badly in an attempt to cover up their fears. Egotism, arrogance, deflection, name-dropping, dismissal of others and pissing contests are a few common examples, but unfortunately, the list goes on and on.

One of the sadder outcomes is when our inadequacies prevent us from maximizing our true brilliance, such as Tom's inability to sustain his leadership position or marry his best friend. We simply see ourselves as not being worthy of the goodness that life has in store for us so we don't seek it, let alone ask for it, or we let our innate strengths and talents stay hidden because we are too afraid that if people see our *not enoughs* they will perceive us as weak overall. We then become our own worst enemies. Leaders must mentally allow for good things to happen to them and around them.

Have you ever experienced any of the following thoughts?

I am not smart enough, talented enough, mathematical enough. I am not educated enough, strong enough, creative enough. I am not lucky enough, courageous enough, likeable enough.

I do not have enough resources, money or influence. I

do not have enough cars, houses or boats. I do not have enough time, energy or respect.

Each of us fills in the blanks with our own limiting perceptions, and these limitations boil down to our personal *not enoughs*.

Our *not enoughs* often haunt us and hurt us, preventing us from actualizing our true talents and gifts. On the flip side, they can drive us to achieve incredible accomplishments, but usually at a high price. We don't seek the accomplishment because we are pursuing a positive passion, we pursue the accomplishment because we lack something, and we falsely believe that achievement will fulfill this lack.

Questioning if we are enough is a ubiquitous feeling in an achievement, accomplishment, keeping-up-with-the-Jones oriented society. Tactically, we can focus on our strengths, hire strong people to bolster our weaknesses, delegate to the accountant or marketing guru, but we often then just ask the same underlying question in a new way. *Am I asking the right questions in this accounting meeting? Do I look stupid? Do I know enough to sound at least halfway intelligent about this marketing campaign or these algorithms?*

There's a myth that great leaders know everything, or at the very least they know a tremendous amount of information about almost everything. We perpetuate this myth with the Renaissance man, with movie heroes and hero-ines who speak multiple languages, defuse bombs, tango dance into the night, break codes in their spare time all the while looking at building schematics for the best pos-sible way to seek revenge upon the bad guys.

In the real world, brilliant leaders have interpreters, trip over their own two feet, have bad breath after they eat garlic bread, misunderstand a concept, lack knowledge in certain domain areas, and still accomplish masterful re-sults. They are enough, just as they are, even when they need a breath mint.

Leaders who engage with others, ask for help, collab-orate effectively, admit their vulnerabilities and ask better questions, reduce their feelings of inadequacy. They con-fidently say, *I'm human, I have an incredible vision, and I need your help to accomplish it and here is why you should help me bring this vision to fruition.*

The world needs diverse talents and passions to meet a plethora of needs and to close multiple gaps. There is a place for each of us to lead, for each of us to serve, and to problem solve. Today, just as we are, we are good enough. In fact, we are better than we think we are!

Shame is the most powerful, master emotion. It's the fear that we're not good enough.

—BRENÉ BROWN

. . .

"You yourself, as much as anybody in the entire universe, deserve your love and affection"

—SIDDHARTHA GAUTAMA

CONCEPTS

- Facing and challenging our fears and feelings of not being "enough"
- Self-compassion
- Breaking through limiting beliefs
- The cost of perceiving ourselves as less-than
- Jealousy among friends
- Hiding our inadequacies
- Insecurity and doubts driving our decision-making

REFLECTING ON YOURS

1. What does your ticker tape say? Fill in the blanks for:
   I'm not _____ enough.
   I do not have enough _____.

2. Take a look at your *not enough* statements. Who might you be if you dropped them? Who or what in your life might "show-up" if you dropped them?

3. What decisions in your life were driven by self-doubt rather than self-confidence?

4. How vulnerable about your inadequacies are you willing to be and with whom?

5. What's your quote?

"We must be
willing to let go
of the life we've
planned, so as to
have the life that is
waiting for us."

–JOSEPH CAMPBELL

ANTON

GLOBAL AMBASSADOR
FOR A NON-PROFIT

REBOUNDIN'

1982. *Calvary Academy* versus *The Spartans*. State championship. Five seconds left in the game. We were down by two. Coach called a timeout. Our high school version of the Villanova-Georgetown game to come.

I don't do drama. Perhaps that's why I find myself in high-conflict crisis areas.

Northern Ireland. South Africa. Cyprus. The Middle East. When people ask where I've been they assume the postcard variety, not the gritty, dust-of-history version that overlays their gloss-finished photo. Sure, you can go on a safari or drop into the green sea, but that's not my itinerary. My itinerary is peace. And if I'm creating peace it means I'm starting with conflict.

Technically, I'm starting with basketball. My roots. But basketball is now my most powerful negotiating tool.

My dad was a talent. Voted *Most Valuable Player* in the state his senior year of high school. Got a picture in the paper palming a basketball in each hand. He was the most skilled player our high school has ever seen, scored 49 points in a single game—reigning champ to this day.

He attended a Division I college on a scholarship. He played well, made it to the first round of the Sweet Sixteen his junior year and entered the respectable field of insurance upon graduation. All along he knew pro-ball was not an option, so he majored in economics and actually studied.

If you ask him today he will tell you that his life is filled with blessings. Beautiful wife, kids, dog, good job. I think if life had tossed him a full-time basketball opportunity, he would have caught it with glee, but then perhaps that is my filter. He became a grandfather last year, and he truly believes that this best defines his success. Over the years basketball was a passion, not an obsession, but he enthusiastically shared his passion with me.

At age four he installed a Nerf basketball hoop in my room despite my mother's protests. Since that induction, I've never gone more than two days without shooting a ball, and that's only because some of the flights these days are insanely long.

I'm a guard. At 6′4″ I'm short. Really short, but tall enough for point guard. And before you bring up Nash ... he's a freak of nature. My dad played the odds and won. Putting me at point, teaching me to see the floor, to break down zones, to strategize seconds before bodies pivoted, allowed me to control the pace and the outcome. We were high school state champs two years in a row. Now I stand in the West Bank, leading one of the first-ever integrated teams from East and West Jerusalem in the prestigious Israeli National Basketball League.

How did a middle-class kid, with more talent than my dad, end up here and not playing pro-ball? Life didn't hand me bas-ketballs—*it threw me curve balls.*

At a young age I discovered that basketball and politics are related, and that players are led by coaches who can be extraordinarily brilliant at setting us up to be winners or losers ... both on and off the court.

Two years before high school I was playing on a regional rec team and doing well, mastering my free throws, building confidence in my lay-ups—until a new kid was recruited. Another guard, only he was destined for the town's private high-school, Calvary Academy, a basketball dominator in our region.

Our rec coach, Coach Layton, had tight connections with

Calvary Academy as an informal scout and feeder of young talent. He developed their pipeline of future players in exchange for use of their gym for his own league. At twelve, this was a cumbersome detail until it affected my playing time. The new kid, whose parents could afford to send him to the private high school, took my place as starter. He also took more than half of my minutes. Basketball wasn't quite as much fun when a dad in insurance and a mom in occasional substitute teaching couldn't afford to buy me game time.

My parents spoke with Coach Layton but it only made things worse. Now I was the non-starter with whiny parents. I was not one to sit back and let life bulldoze over me. I felt that a great injustice needed to be righted. I sat down with my father and presented my plan. As his favorite and only son he backed me one-hundred percent.

My dad met with our local public high school boy's varsity coach, Coach Higgins, who led the Spartans to state championships a few years back. They agreed it was a good time to start our own rec team. As point guard for the Bulldogs, named in honor of our forward's dearly departed best friend, we soundly beat Coach Layton's team at every tournament for the next two years. At 13, victory was sweet salve to my lower class wounds.

At 18, I was on my way to Division I. Well, in my mind that is. I dreamed of college scholarships and stardom. I dreamed of being the big man on campus. And I had the discipline and skill to make it happen. To me, it was a sure thing, a done deal.

And I rode in on my chariot of confidence to the 1982 Championship against Calvary Academy.

It was a battle that night. No team ever led by more than four points. Our center fouled out with one minute left in the game. Coach Higgins was beside himself and almost drew a technical, but our assistant coach, Gary, blocked his path to the ref at the last second, or we would surely have watched defeat being snatched from the jaws of victory.

Multiple time-outs were called by both teams, silent hushes from the crowd were followed by bursts of insane cheering as one team and then another scored. Both coaches screaming, "Do not foul! Do not foul!" And then there it was … five seconds left in the game. We were down by two. Coach called our last timeout. In the huddle, he turned to me, and asked one simple question. "Can you deliver?" I nodded. This was my moment. "Yes, Sir!" I remember shouting out with a force that excited and frightened me. We would inbound the ball from the sideline.

We had just enough time. The game plan was for me to throw the ball to Dwayne, and then Dwayne would unexpectedly pass it back to me once I was in-bounds. Everyone would be expecting Dwayne to pass it to one of our tall forwards, Eric or Jermaine. I would take three steps, set and then shoot the three-pointer. Coach repeated the plan and then asked me to repeat it back. I did. He nodded, his lips tight. He looked at Dwayne and asked him to repeat the plan. Dwayne recited my words verbatim. We all put our hands in the middle and shouted, "Spartans!" in our deepest, newly developed, adult voices.

I walked to the sidelines and out of the corner of my eye I saw Coach Layton in the stands for Calvary Academy. I turned and locked eyes with him. He nodded and smirked, and I shook my head clear as I watched in slow motion as the ref put the whistle in his mouth before handing me the ball. Trevor, No. 29 from Calvary Academy, was in my face, waving his arms wildly. Their No. 16, a huge guy, was shoving his elbow into Dwayne's rib cage, but the refs weren't calling anything now. This was it. Dwayne stepped right, the big guy followed, and then Dwayne shifted left and the big guy couldn't change his weight's momentum fast enough and that was our split second opportunity. I threw hard to Dwayne and immediately raced for the three-point line. Dwayne caught it, dribbled twice, and then called out Eric's name super loud at the exact same moment he threw it to me on the opposite side of the court. I caught the ball, took three steps, set my stance and took the shot.

All I remember hearing was the buzzer ringing in my ear as I watched the slow arc of the ball and then, as if the whole convention center was silent, I heard the sweet swoosh as the ball lowered cleanly through the net. Pandemonium ensued. We won! We were victors by a single shot. My throat clamped shut, working overtime to prevent me from crying. The euphoria was all consuming. Every fiber of my being radiated joy. State Champs!

Five days later I was diagnosed with testicular cancer. My world was rocked. My dreams shifted overnight. My vocabulary did too. *Jump-shot, lay-up, chest-pass, in the zone* were replaced by *real shots, laid-up, passed-out* and *in over my head.* One phrase translated well: *personal foul.*

When I was supposed to be talking to scouts and coaches and selecting from the best of multiple scholarship offers I was talking to oncologists and radiologists, waiting for test results, and determining treatment plans. It didn't take long for a Stage II seminoma diagnosis to be returned. The cancer had spread to a nearby lymph node.

Surgery and chemo replaced prom. I let my date down easy. By May the chemo made me bald, discolored my skin, deflated my ego, and my left hand was numb. She said she understood, it was really okay, she wished me well and went with our high school's quarterback.

The college scouts were no different. They said they understood, it was really okay, get well, let us know if you get feeling back in your hand, and they signed with other talented players.

I hit the wall. I descended. At 18 I felt like I was done being a basketball player—done being a man. I lost energy, I lost enthusiasm, I lost strength, *I lost me.*

And then one Saturday morning when I was feeling sorry for myself I turned on the television and saw a small boy, age six or seven, fleeing from his home. He was on fire. A Molotov cocktail had been thrown through the front window of his home. And there I was sitting in a safe, clean family room feeling sorry for myself.

Something shifted in my brain. To this day I'm not exactly sure of the science behind it, but I will tell you with pure sincerity that I felt that switch in my head. I felt it in my whole body.

I had a disease that would probably be cured. The kid on TV had an affliction that would maim him for life if it didn't kill him. I lived in the greatest country in the history of the world. That kid lived in a dangerous hell-hole, if he still lived at all.

I can't imagine living where you wake up every day and know someone will be shot, that someone you personally know, that your neighbor knows, that your cousin knows, will be dead by sunset. It's a concept that I cannot wrap my head around.

I grew more concerned about that TV kid than my own cancer. I could see his eyes while the fire singed his skin.

I looked into the future that morning, and I envisioned him as a man driven by hostility toward those who would have killed him. I could see a never-ending cycle of revenge. I wanted to scream that a small boy would be filled with a hatred he was not born with, and yet who would blame him? He wouldn't just snack on hatred, it would fuel his daily life. He and his family would be filled with animosity toward those responsible for his injuries. His family would encourage him to get even. That's the way much of the world now operates, but it doesn't have to.

The picture of that TV kid changed my life. I understood all too well that life could turn on a dime. Because of the TV kid, I started strategizing both offensively and defensively about how I could use my skills to maximize my healing—and his. I was on a new journey—a detour. My destination was the same, but my path was now a new life. My primary goal was to beat cancer, evaluate where I was and then figure out what I wanted to do with my life for his.

That's when one of my doctors introduced me to a basketball program that encourages kids to play ball for peace.

One of the doctors treating me said he too had played basketball in high school. He was good enough to get an athletic scholarship. However, he lived on a farm, and after his senior year he was helping his dad and his jeans got caught in the teeth of the tractor. He lost his left leg. His basketball days were over. The school honored his scholarship and he went on to be an Interventional Radiologist. The story stuck in his throat, but when he gave it voice he said it changed him and his life for the better. As horrible as it was, he shared, the loss of his leg caused him to pursue a profession he believed he would not have pursued otherwise. In some ways the injury turned out to be a blessing. It was a certainly a blessing to me. He was wicked smart, and helped my body beat cancer. I owe him my life. That is not drama. That is a fact.

I had surgery, radiation and chemo. In that order. It took nine months. I did not start college as planned and I did not play basketball as planned. But I graduated with honors five years later, double majoring in Middle-Eastern Studies and Psychology.

I believe I am making a difference as I watch young children from warring factions learn teamwork, strategy, conflict-resolution, and build bonds of friendship. Bonds that they take back to their communities. Bonds that will help tomorrow's generation play better.

And if you think these high-conflict areas are beyond redemption—that one man cannot change the world—then picture a small boy playing outside his home, drawing in the dirt with a stick. Tonight, for once, he will go to bed safely. He will sleep peacefully. Tomorrow the sun will dawn a new day, there will be no Molotov cocktails, there will be no deaths, his family will not fuel hatred and revenge.

Some say I'm looking too far ahead. They don't know me. Twelve years ago I was a leader in high school. I led the basketball team to the state title. How many people do you know who won the state championship with the final shot? I am a survivor. I am an ambassador for peace.

◂▾▸

Exploring Leaders' **Secrets**

Life is an endurance test. How we respond to life's trials, tribulations and idiosyncrasies is a choice. Accepting responsibility for our choices and decisions about our thoughts, feelings and actions allows us to own our story. Leaders who remain calm and focus on what *can* be controlled and the choices that can still be made, reduce their stress levels and open doors that yield more opportunities. Leaders who replace furious with curious, reinvent the next part of their lives even bigger and bolder.

Like Anton, how we choose to overcome challenges of all kinds—trauma, tragedy, personal and professional crises, disappointments, set-backs—reveals our inner strength and influences our outer actions. If we can lead ourselves through these many crises we are better equipped to lead others. Our leadership is shaped by our life experiences—especially the experiences that teach us lessons the hard way.

While steering through adversity requires many skills and traits such as optimism, creativity as problem-solving and adaptability (to name a few), there are two critical mental mindsets that are imperative for successfully surviving adversity: (1) our learning agility and (2) staying calm and focused on what we *can* control and the choices we *can* still make.

Without pain there truly is no gain. Our ability to find

95

the gain in the pain and apply that gain going forward demonstrates our learning agility. Leaders who look at a loss, a setback, or a failure, and ask, *"What am I learning from this adversity? How do I apply my learnings to the next setback?"* or *"How might I apply this lesson to prevent the next challenge?"* transform their knowledge into wisdom.

We are born with a strong will to survive. When we respond to adverse conditions by recalibrating and realigning inner direction with outward service we remain heroes of our own lives. Some of us know how to lead at a young age. Others find that we are leaders later in life. Either way, when we are able to bounce back stronger, wiser, and more powerful, our potential to lead expands exponentially. Being able to bounce back requires openness to new possibilities, to new choices, to a new *how*. Leaders who set a vision and big goals, but then create room for a flexible, adaptable *how* are often more successful in realizing their goals or visions because while they keep the end in mind, they are open to how best to move toward these goals.

Inversely, sometimes a goal itself is unattainable, requiring leaders to recalibrate their vision by manifesting their passion and purpose in a new way or choosing a new passion and purpose all together. Both Anton and the Radiologist created new paths: Anton retaining his passion for basketball and playing a variation of the game as an ambassador for peace, and the Radiologist finding an entirely new passion and purpose in medicine. All of these adaptations require faith that there will be a solution when one isn't immediately evident. This faith in tomorrow's solution requires faith in oneself—believing that you still have value and that there is still a sacred, unique place to shine your light.

"Things turn out best for the
people who make the best of
the way things turn out."

–JOHN WOODEN

• • •

"Adversity introduces a
man to himself."

–ALBERT EINSTEIN

CONCEPTS

- Resiliency
- Facing adversity
- Strength of character
- Not letting our failures or successes define us
- Charting our course despite unexpected events
- No pain no gain

REFLECTING ON YOURS

1. Where has loss, disappointment or tragedy impacted your life?

2. How well do you handle setbacks?

3. How are you converting your pain into gain?

4. Have you ever not been resilient, succumbing for a time to life's unexpected disappointments or crises?

5. Where in your own life do you believe setbacks are still holding you captive (socially, economically, mentally, emotionally, spiritually, politically)?

6. How might you best prepare for what's next in your life?

◂ ▴ ▸

"You'll never change the world if you're always worried about being liked."

—ROBIN SHARMA

TRISH

VP OF MARKETING

Bein' Likeable

Talking to a stranger at a bar:

I was at Happy Hour last week with my creative director, Joe. Five-dollar well drinks and the best pot stickers in town—amazing ponzu sauce. Joe was with his new girlfriend Samantha. When Joe introduced us, you know what the first words out of her mouth were? "You smell like lemon cleaner."

Now, don't get me wrong, I can call 'em as I see 'em too—well at least in our ad campaigns I can—and I pride myself on that. That's what got me where I am today. Just got a promotion last week—Senior VP of Marketing—it's why we were out celebrating.

Oh, thanks! Yeah, I am excited. Bit nervous too.

Tonight? No, not celebrating tonight. This glass of wine is called "Zen the nervous Nellies." Blind date—I'm early.

Where was I? Oh yes—I'll admit it might have been true; I was trying out a new fragrance and it did smell a bit … citrusy perhaps. But lemon cleaner? I'm sorry, there's a huge difference between constructive criticism and being just plain ole mean. I took the high road though, just smiled. Because that's what I do. Number One: I'm nice. I believe in always being nice. And Number Two: I'm positive, downright optimistic. Studies have shown that an optimistic mindset actually generates more ideas, better ideas. We even know that a sense of optimism leads to longer life expectancy. Literally, words to live by.

And then half-way through our lettuce-wraps—did I mention our instant dislike, her for me, I could tell from the moment we shook hands—half way through our lettuce-wraps she says, "You smell like floor wax." What?! Because I was being nice she thinks I'm stupid and didn't understand her the first time? Nice does not mean naïve. You had me at lemon cleaner, lady—I was just taking the high road.

"New perfume," I responded. You know what she said? "You

smell like my cleaning lady." So now she's insulting me and her cleaning lady? That cleaning lady scrubs her dried poo out of toilets—how about showing her a little respect, right?

If she must say it, how about, "That perfume isn't the best. You might let it go." And while we're at it, how about, "Thank you, cleaning lady, for exposing yourself to cleaning chemicals regularly for my benefit." And just for the record, my cleaning lady has a name, Rosa, and she makes wickedly good empanadas and smells like my Grandma.

I couldn't tell if she was trying to make me feel bad, make me self—conscious, make me leave to go shower—all I know is it was rude. And I can hear her now, saying to her girl-friends, "Dumb blonde didn't even understand that I was insulting her."

I have this fantasy where I take someone down with the perfect come-back. "Smell like lemon cleaner, eh?! At least that's better than smelling like a horse's—oh, you get the picture. One day, just one time, I'd like to say *to heck with the high road—I'm taking the low road like a monster truck!* But nope—my grandmother taught me better. "Know better, do better," she'd say. "Be kind, Patricia." Sometimes it's maddening to know better.

Hey, can I have another Chardonnay, best buddy Bartender Mike? Pleases and thank yous. No, not this one, a more buttery one? Great—thanks.

On second thought, that should be my Number Two motto in life—be a peace-keeper.

So let me re-phrase then: Number One: *I'm nice.* Number Two: *I'm a peace-keeper.* And Number Three: *I'm optimistic.* That's me. That's my deal. I want everything to be hunky-dory. Avoid conflict at all costs. Channel Gandhi—that's my motto; but this can be easier said than done. It takes quite a bit of energy to avoid conflict actually, because frankly, people say the stupidest things.

I know they mean well, most of the time—unlike Samantha—which is why I'm great at ferrying buts over faux pas and smoothing things out. But honestly, good intentions can come out wrong. Just last month my cousin got diagnosed with breast cancer. One of her dearest friends said, "Better you than me."

I know! A totally idiotic thing to say, I'll give you that, but my cousin is incredibly strong, so grounded. I think that's what this woman was trying to say, but it sure came out wrong. So I shared this perspective and my cousin immediately felt better. Didn't excuse the horrific comment, just made it easier to understand, and hopefully forgive. That would be my Number Four, *helping people feel better.*

That was followed three days later by my friend's dad's funeral. I'd never been to a Jewish funeral. The Rabbi was about five minutes into his speech when even he acknowledged that people will say the darnedest things. "So forgive them," he said. "Ignore them," he encouraged. I think he knew what was coming. Not ten minutes later my friend's sister is saying how their mom was the love of their dad's life. No mind that they divorced years ago and that he'd remarried. Or that his now wife of a gazillion years is sitting there crying. She followed that foot in her mouth with a story about how their father attended Mandarin cooking classes only to pick up Chinese chicks. Because why else would a Jewish man want Chinese food? Um, I don't know, maybe because he likes orange chicken and he teaches English to non-native speakers at the community college who just stepped off the boat from Beijing?!

And so what did I do? I smoothed it over. I told my friend's sister her remarks were heartfelt, that they reflected her loss for family. Which is true. I told my friend her sister did the best she could with limited brain cells. That's also true, her sister is not the sharpest knife in the drawer—I just didn't say that to her sister. My ability to put a high gloss veneer over the truth has served me well, but I think it might be eroding my insides. Maybe I'm channeling Dorian Gray by mistake.

Thanks, Mike.

Ahhhh ... yes, much better; less grapefruit, more buttery. Perfect—thank you.

My therapist says I'm giving my power away when I walk an enabler's tightrope. I sorta knew what she meant, but she explained it as not calling people on their rubbish. I love that euphemism, my grandmother's favorite replacement for a cuss word—*rubbish*. I told my therapist that I tell the truth all the time, compassionately, sometimes with gilt-framing and kid gloves. She said I'm nice because I'm afraid people will dislike me. Too much seeking of external validation apparently. She asked me, *Would it be so bad if your cousin told her friend her insensitive comment hurt her feelings? Would it be so terrible if my friend shared with her sister that her remarks hurt their mother's feelings?*

I struggle with this. What comes of it? Who would be your friend? Who would want to hang with you if you said, *You're being an idiot.* Apparently this question is exactly what makes me an A+ enabler. Hi, my name is Trish, and I want you to like me, like me, like me. I'm seeking your smile as validation that all is right with me. And here's my scary new thought: I think trying hard to be liked has gotten me where I am today, but I don't think it's going to work in my new position. I see signs already that it may be a bad habit. It may not get me what I need. I have this precarious feeling I'm about to know better, but on this one, it's going to be crazy hard to do better. I think I might be addicted to being nice.

I told my friend's sister she gave a brilliant eulogy. Technically, a brilliant job at making her step-mother feel like dirt and her sisters want to strangle her, but I just smiled, hugged her and said her father would be proud. Why did I have to say anything? Why didn't I just walk away, grab a bagel, shalom a few folks and be done with it?! Because I'm nice. Only I think I'm now confusing nice with downright lying.

In real life, it's hard to be truthful and be liked. On television, it's easy to be snarky and liked. I won three awards last year for this hilarious ad campaign on women versus men drivers. Our client's sales actually went up 12% during our ad series. Just couldn't tell my boyfriend at the time that I got my material from him. When he saw one of the ads I had to fess up though—it was blatantly him. Is that truth-telling serving me well? No—definitely not. I mean professionally—absolutely. Hellooo?? Three statues sit on my mantel, but the dude is gone.

Honestly? I'm a little too good at avoiding the truth in order to keep the status quo. I want to be the good guy. I want to be the one everyone likes. I can't stand conflict—so *not* a fan. You know, the unvarnished truth isn't always well received. Do you think for one minute if Meryl Streep—love her by the way, huge fan—if Meryl actually said out loud, "*You driving twenty-something with your crease-free face and perky chest, please do not mention what an honor it is to be nominated along side me when you accept your Oscar,*" we'd still love her? Nope, the media would call her a monster, a horrible person, but she's probably thought it. And that just makes her human. It's weird. We don't want our role models to be human. We want them to be super-heroes. In fact, when they seem a little too much like us, we tend to like them less. Sad.

Maybe it is me I'm more worried about. Maybe I can't handle someone's awful reactions to the truth. What do you do with somebody else's rage or hurt, or melodrama? It's easier to be kind and know they're going to be just fine. Nobody's going to get hurt.

I think it's why I've gotten promoted so quickly. Everybody loves me. I make people feel good about themselves.

Hey, you're pretty cute. Your name isn't Dave by any chance is it? I'm supposed to be meeting a guy named Dave.

Cameron? That's a nice name. Very solid. Gaelic. Means "crooked nose" if I remember correctly. Your nose is straight. Hi, Cameron. Trish. Nice to meet you. I'm meeting this Dave guy. Blind date. He's now late. Obviously.

I'm starving though and this second glass is going straight to my head. Hey, best buddy Bartender Mike, can I have some pretzels? Please? Or maybe some bread? Something? Anything? More alms for the poor please! Thanks!

What was I saying? Oh yes, everybody loves me. Well, except for Samantha.

What do *you* think was up with floor-wax Sam? Jealous? Or maybe just threatened. Threatened! That's the deal, right there!

Everyone tells women to be confident, Cameron; they invite us to "lean in," to follow our dreams, to not take no for an answer. So we do, we lean in, we're bold, we go after stuff. And guess what? They hate us for it. They're threatened by us! Apparently, it turns out, a lot of women don't really like other super-confident women. Be strong! Slay those dragons without a Prince! Break that glass ceiling! Leap over those hurdles! Wait, you did all that? Oh my goodness … you're such an aggressive, overly-ambitious be-yotch!

They don't say it, but the "b" word hides in the word ambitious when we use it to describe women. "She's … ambitious." Wink, nudge, eyebrow arch.

"You know what I mean, Cameron? Am-be-yotch-ous?" No, bad pun, forget it, it doesn't work.

Ah, bread! Just in time! Thanks, Mike. You're a lifesaver. Help yourself, Cameron. Please. There's enough bread here to sink a battleship. And this butter! It's whipped with orange-blossom honey. Makes you want to smear it right into your arteries.

For the love of God people can make you want to escape.

Oh you have to go? Is it that late? Hmmm, sorry to keep you, *Cameron*—I didn't realize you had dinner plans elsewhere! Just give me one more second please, hear me out— women have to be likeable. That's the belief. A man can be a drill sergeant, treat his team like if they don't keep up he's going to vote them off the island, and people still fight to glean his wisdom. But a woman? Approachable. Likeable. *Nice.* We need to show chinks in our armor. We have to show that we're vulnerable. And only then do people like us. They tell us to be ambitious but they praise us for being nice instead.

And who doesn't want to be liked?! Right? I do. Can I be honest? I want to be liked. But I don't see it working now. How can I be in charge and be nice?

Hey, I'm smart, I work my tail off, and like I said, being nice has probably helped, but where does that leave me? If I'm not nice, then they won't promote me, but in order to really lead I'm going to have to draw some lines in the sand, I'm going to have to create boundaries, I'm going to have to say and do things that aren't very nice at all.

Do I have to start faking chinks in my armor so my team doesn't think I'm a total ball-buster? Do I still smile at floor wax Samantha, thank her for letting me know I'm lemon-fresh? Or do I now say to her, "I understand that you're insulting me. I see that you're in some way triggered, but please, let's try to pass the evening in some more pleasant way…" but then I'm the shrew! See how that works?

Or you—if I'd said to you, "Actually, *Dave*, I'd guessed that your name wasn't really Cameron even before I'd been able to sneak a look at your bar tab," then somehow I'd be the one who was out of line—as opposed to the person who was lying about their name to get out of a blind date.

No, no—no need to apologize. I understand. Really I do.

Second apology accepted. No, I'm fine, truly. Thanks. Yea, you too.

Yep, Mike, that *was* blind date Dave. It's maddening, Mike, I just accepted that jerk's apologies sweetly because I still want to be liked. He was dissing me, on his way out the door under a *pseudonym*, and I still wanted him to like me. What's wrong with me? Why can't I just say, "*You're a jerk dude, and not a very covert one at that?*"

I'm scared, Mike.

No, I'm serious. I just got promoted to VP, and I think it's just starting to dawn on me that my grandmother's "be kind" is not the same as "be nice" … and while *Webster* says they're synonyms, what if they aren't at all when it comes to putting them into action? What if success has nothing to do with being nice but with being kind? What if that means I have to start acting in a likeable way but stop caring if they actually like me?! Yikes … I am so not there yet. Can I stand up for myself, be truthful, and still be successful? Meaning, will people eventually still like me? Ugh!!!

Here I am having a meal of bread and butter in my favorite bar, and feeling dumb about not making it to the appetizer, simply because I find it impossible to walk the line between being honest and being likeable. See how well that worked? I got dumped before the first date.

Wait, what? Say that again. Do I want to have dinner with you? Aw, no, Mike, very sweet of you, but I don't need your pity date.

Really … you've wanted to ask me for months? Refreshingly charming?! Ha! Really? Are you messing with me?

No?

Wow. I did not see this coming. Man. I have so much to learn.

◂ ▾ ▸

Exploring Leaders' **Secrets**

Most of us would rather be liked than not liked. We do not typically wake up in the morning and say, *"What can I do today to earn the disregard and distaste of my followers?"* However, when leaders focus too much on being liked, they cannot lead effectively.

When we focus on being liked, we unconsciously attempt to please the people we're leading, and people pleasing can lead to a lack of clarity, integrity and truth about what we stand for, where we're going and why. People pleasing alienates followers and fractures the group, reaping the exact opposite of what we are trying to do—and that is, gather people together for a common cause, a common goal, a common destination. Like Trish, when we focus on being liked, we lose the courage to say what needs to be said or do what needs to done. This lack of courage generates missed opportunities and yields diluted results.

Trish realizes that her lack of courage is no longer working, in fact, it's "eroding her insides." While she's very new in her leadership role, she is already aware that she will need to transition her focus from *being liked* to *leading*. As her grandmother pointed out, leaders must be kind, even when it is painful, even when the low road would be easier, but we do so because we are leading, role-modeling how people should be treated, not yearning to be liked. Focusing on leading does not require leaders to abandon kindness. Behaving in a likeable manner, showing mercy, offering forgiveness, and demonstrating self-respect conveys leadership and yields results—a bonus, ironic byproduct is that others often like us more when we're focused on leading instead of worrying about likeability.

One of the boomerang effects of wanting everyone to like us is that we end up not liking ourselves. By compromising on our values, telling too many white-lies, pretending to be something or someone we're not, or not standing up for ourselves, we sell a piece of ourselves until there's nothing left to respect in the way of self-respect.

When leaders focus on connecting with others' interests and needs instead of attempting to connect via contrived or artificial compliments; when leaders acknowledge and validate real feelings—in ourselves and in others—instead of avoiding or dismissing them; and when leaders maintain integrity in their words and actions, instead of trying to be everything to all people; those that follow them will do so because they believe in the leader and the ultimate mission.

"Effective leadership is not about making speeches or being liked; leadership is defined by results, not attributes."

–PETER DRUCKER

• • •

"If you set out to be liked, you would be prepared to compromise on anything at any time, and you would achieve nothing."

–MARGARET THATCHER

CONCEPTS

- The need to be liked
- Role of likeability in leadership
- Learning how to integrate truth with kindness
- Standing up for ourselves
- Like versus respect
- Choosing likeability over conflict

REFLECTING ON YOURS

1. How much do you want others to like you?

2. What do you do or say to avoid friction or confrontation in your life?

3. Is disliking and avoiding conflict a barrier to effective leadership?

4. To what degree do you "go along" so as to "get along" and fail to stand up for yourself?

5. How focused are you on being liked versus leading?

6. Can a leader be disliked and still be respected?

"The system wants you to be either a bow or an arrow; refuse both, because there is a third choice: to be an archer!"

–MEHMET MURAT ILDAN, Playwright

HUSTON

RETIRED

BUCKIN' THE SYSTEM

THE YEAR WAS 1964. Civil Rights was a daily headline. They called me a *nigger lover*.

When I first heard these words they didn't fully register. Somewhere in my brain I was smart enough to not say *Huh?*, to avoid hearing them spoken out loud again that day, but the sound of those words forever reverberate within me.

I would hear them again externally over the next few months. Sometimes in mumbled slurs, sometimes more openly, more aggressively; and sometimes they would hint at what they were calling me without coming right out and saying the words.

You an oreo lover? You shouldn't help him. Heard you had dinner with him. Blockbuster. Being his friend will hurt your career. Stay friends with that monkey and you won't be on my committee.

Lloyd was the first African American my government agency hired. He was a 35-year-old programmer trained in Cobol. He made the Senior Managers fidgety. They liked having their shoes shined—and their shoes were shined by a black man named Flinty who rarely spoke. Lloyd, on the other hand, liked to talk, and not only did he want to talk, he wanted to talk like colleagues, like equals. To them, it wasn't right. To me, we were just two men with more in common than our differences and a shared passion for sports.

What wasn't right to Lloyd was that Flinty was also the Senior Managers' chauffer. Monday through Friday, Flinty dropped head honchos off at power lunches and brought them back to their offices at two in the afternoon, too inebriated to actually function.

But on Sundays, Flinty was the pastor of a Baptist church in Landover, Maryland, just a bit northeast of the D.C. line off Martin Luther King Jr. Boulevard. What Lloyd wanted to know one day at lunch was, "How can a Pastor, a disciple of

God and leader of precious souls, shine the shoes of these prejudiced knuckle-heads?"

I shrugged. It was technically a rhetorical question. But I understood. And I understood that Lloyd wanted to do something about it. And he did.

Lloyd was smart. So bright, that upper management enjoyed discrediting him whenever possible. In those days, BASIC was the programming language of choice. It was designed for idiot savants, so the managers assumed anyone and everyone who knew programming, knew BASIC. But Lloyd did not. He preferred programming with Cobol, a much more sophisticated, advanced programming code that left BASIC users in the dust. But to the managers, with their complete lack of programming knowledge, Lloyd was the idiot who could not even program a simple line of *BASIC*. No matter how many times I attempted to explain that they were misinformed, that Cobol was actually a different, more sophisticated language, they would raise their hand dismissively, too busy to be bothered with a rational, sound explanation.

Not only was Lloyd the very first African American to be hired in my agency, he was hired as a Grade 13. This grade was a very threatening position of potential—potentially a peer, potentially a job taker, potentially a boss. The fear on these managers' faces was real. They could not possibly end their 30-year careers in government working with, let alone for, a black man.

After Lloyd and I settled into a routine of eating lunch

together and playing backgammon on Friday's, he invited my family to his home for dinner. I didn't hesitate. Yes. Absolutely. Lloyd was a thinker, and I appreciated his company. The following Saturday I took my wife Ruth and our four kids out to have supper with Lloyd, his wife Sally, and their two daughters. I can't recall all that happened that night, but I do recall that my daughter Liz was stunned to see a painting of Jesus as a black man and that all baby dolls weren't white. I still smile remembering when she shared her startling discovery in the car on the way home and Ruth saying, "Well, what did you think Lizzy, that black people have white babies?"

'Was Jesus black?" Lizzy asked.

"Probably a bit more sun-tanned than our Casper version," Ruth replied sardonically.

And therein Lizzy's world-view tilted. Jesus was not perhaps as white as her children's Bible had led her to believe, and the world made black baby dolls. I think her head was actually spinning. Today she works with Bank of America's Global Ambassador program. She's a go-getter that one. Made of solid stuff.

The Monday following our dinner, Lloyd met with Flinty. Told the minister if he didn't quit shining shoes he would show up at his church and share the truth with his congregation. He'd share with them that while Flinty preached to them about not being bound, not being suppressed, he himself was tending to the soles of oppressors instead of respecting his own soul. It was a pretty moving speech. When he re-delivered it to me later that afternoon in the lunchroom I could easily envision Flinty seeing his flock shaking their heads in displeasure. I think Flinty could also envision empty offering plates, so by Wednesday it was over. No more shoe-shining and a lot more pissed-off managers. One in particular—Reed Johnson. My boss.

To say that Reed was rattled would be like saying that Bernie, our St. Bernard, drools a little. We keep towels in every room. When Reed's full-blown temper tantrum ratcheted down a notch he noticed my shoes were unlaced.

"What's with your laces, Huston?"

"I prefer to wear my shoes unlaced, Sir."

"That's not our policy."

"I know, Sir. I still prefer to wear unlaced shoes."

"You will lace your shoes or I will write you up for insubordination. Do you understand what I'm saying? This is the United States government, Son."

"Yes, Sir."

And with that, Reed Johnson was gone from my office, and white man's belief in his supremacy and power to stop a changing world was going to rest upon the size of my bunny-eared double knots.

At about the same time that African Americans like Lloyd were causing enough trouble to "threaten" the state of my laces, so was the middle class. Everyone seemed to want equality that week.

The second revolution started with SES lunches.

The Senior Executive Service, known as SES, was created to "…ensure that the executive management of the Government of the United States is responsive to the needs, policies, and goals of the Nation and otherwise is of the highest quality."

SES executives are all that's left at the top after General Schedule grades, and they are the major link between political appointees and the rest of the Federal workforce. They operate and oversee nearly every government activity in approximately 75 Federal agencies, and they were allowed to bring lunches from home. Why? Because they had refrigerators bought and paid for by you and I. While they could indeed bring lunches, they did not, preferring to go to the Officer's club where martinis were cheap. Suffice it to say, their refrigerators were empty except for the occasional clandestine bottle of wine.

Murmurs of refrigerator unrest amongst the middle class government workers began. SES' disregard and contempt of perfectly good refrigerators was baffling to us GSers. We craved to bring lunches from home that required refrigeration. I too had visions of leftover meatloaf sandwiches dancing in my head instead of peanut butter and banana. We GSers decided to get our own refrigerator.

I coordinated a meeting in Frank Howell's office at 2pm the following Tuesday. Meanwhile, Tom was assigned to call refrigerator sales ads in the Virginia area, I took ads in the District, and Martin was tasked with Bethesda. Marcia would survey our agency employees to collect a small contribution from all who wanted to participate.

The following Tuesday it was determined that Tom had located the best deal in Fredericksburg, Virginia. I agreed to drive down there with him, and Marcia reported that all 23 people in our agency wanted to participate. *Operation Mayonnaise* was a go.

Saturday dawned bright and sunny and Tom and I were actually feeling a bit daring as we headed down Interstate 95: two government employees, GS-12, flipping the bird to SESers and their "Private SES Use Only" refrigerators.

At the end of a very long dirt road, behind free roaming chickens and a barn stood our hero.

"The ad didn't say she was Pepto Bismol pink," Tom muttered, red rising up his face.

"I don't care," I replied. "She's huge. Twenty-three lunches will fit with some room to spare." I tapped gently on her left side and a small piece of rusted metal fell to the side. I opened the door, and the hinges glided open and closed without a squeak. She looked ghastly but seemed to function.

"Does she really work?" Tom asked her owner. He spit and then nodded.

"It's official government business," Tom said sternly, quickly flashing his zero-authority ID card. "I don't want to have to come back tomorrow and arrest you for false advertising," he warned.

The owner shook his head. "She works perfectly. Just too big for us." Tom hesitated, nodded, handed him $30 and we loaded her onto his truck.

Everyone was ecstatic that for $1.30 each (I threw in the extra dime) we were now the proud owners of our own agency refrigerator. We nicknamed her Bismo, and she filled up fast. To say that morale skyrocketed would be like saying Larry Bird knew how to dribble. Bismo was our favorite new team member for exactly four days before word got out that we had purchased our own fridge.

The first complaint was filed the following Wednesday by a different agency down the hall. They declared that having "a non-government fridge utilizing government-funded electricity was an abusive use of our power." No pun intended by this letter, but for which we all found highly amusing and annoying. We called a lunch meeting to address this issue. I had not even had one bite of my meatloaf sandwich when Marcia arrived smiling.

"I found a loophole," she declared.

Twenty-two pairs of eyebrows rose expectantly.

"It says we can absolutely have a personal-use refrigerator supported by government electricity if one of the government employees uses it to store diabetic insulin."

It took us exactly 38 minutes to find our diabetic. Technically, in another agency, but the rules didn't get that specific. Round 1 was declared a victory.

The second complaint was filed two weeks after we received our government issued medical refrigerator certificate. We displayed it proudly … the certificate, not the complaint. The Building Service Managers wanted use of our fridge and said they had a right to it as their office was in our same building. We all agreed that while it would be nice to share, we didn't have enough room for 15 more lunches, and if we opened it to the Building Service Managers we would open the floodgates to every agency in the building and that the refrigerator we had bought with our own money might not even be available for our use. The Building Service Managers took our decision and their appeal to SES.

SES, not giving a second's consideration to their multiple empty refrigerators, gave a direct order to our agency to share our fridge immediately. The same day that the other agency employees were granted permission to use our refrigerator, our lunches started disappearing. At first, everyone was too polite to accuse one another of out right stealing, but over the course of weeks, no matter how boldly you wrote your name on your brown bag, your lunch simply vanished.

And then one day I physically caught someone munching my meal. I walked straight into the lunchroom to find one of the Building Service Managers munching happily on my meatloaf sandwich.

"That's mine!" I cried out.

"Prove it," he snarled.

I pointed to my name in huge letters written on the crumpled brown bag. "Huston. That's my name!"

He shrugged and pulled out the last saliva sodden bite from his mouth. "Here you go."

We gathered at 9am the following morning. Everyone was

incensed but there were no viable solutions. Going against SES was not a battle we would win. We left discouraged.

The next day Fred from Building Services was found to be groaning in the men's bathroom. He went home early. Martin lit matches in the offending stall.

The following day Larry from Building Services threw up in the hallway, annoying his fellow maintenance managers who had to clean it up.

Friday, Greg from Building Services had diarrhea so bad he had to go home for clean pants. Building Services immediately called a meeting with our agency and accused us of poisoning them. I waved them off. "You guys are insane," I said. "No one's poisoning you. The flu's going around and you all have it."

"Actually … ," a soft voice tentatively made itself heard. I turned to see Henry Mitten, all 5'2" of him, pull himself upright and stick out his chin. "They sort of have been poisoned."

There was a collective gasp. "What?"

"I crushed my wife's laxative pills into powder and sprinkled it into the mayonnaise," he said, not one wit sorry. "They've been stealing our food. They've denied it, but there's no denying it now."

Everyone looked from Henry to the fridge to the Building Service Managers and back to Henry. Round 2 was a quasi-victory, as we were validated in our accusations about theft, since they were caught red-handed, or more like brown-bottomed, but everyone threw away their lunches just to be safe.

Victory was short-lived. The next morning we arrived to find our refrigerator bolted shut. They had actually drilled holes through the door and padlocked it. Building Service Managers were the only ones with the keys. When we complained to SES they reprimanded us for poisoning our fellow employees and said they didn't blame Building Services for feeling the need to protect their food. "Poisoning" another employee was a federal offense, and there were rumors that they might bring Henry up on charges.

Reed Johnson paid me a visit. "Henry Mitton work for you?"

"No, Sir."

"Who on earth does he work for?"

"He's your direct report, Sir."

"Oh." He looked under the desk. "Dang-nabbit, Huston, I told you to start tying your shoes."

"Yes, Sir."

"Are you going to tie them or do I need to really write you up?"

I appreciated his compound questions. If he ever just asked me the first part I might have to lie. "No, Sir, you do not need to write me up."

"Good!"

Lloyd and I were back to peanut butter and banana sandwiches when Marcia posted a memo above the coffee maker later that afternoon. It read: "Coffee—35¢ per cup starting Monday."

"What's going on?" I inquired.

"Reed's charging for coffee."

"Why?" Lloyd asked.

"Our Sunshine fund has run out of cash and there have been so many complaints about dirty pots and which agency is not contributing money to the fund that he's decided we need a new system. They're installing a fancy dispensing machine over the weekend and charging per cup."

I looked at Lloyd. We were having a similar reaction. It was typical of SESers to make changes about us and for us without ever consulting us.

"So now we're paying even more for coffee," Lloyd mumbled out loud.

"Yep," Marcia rolled her eyes. "Lucky us."

She was a beauty. I have to admit it. Lloyd even whistled when we saw our new coffee dispenser. Tom was just pissed.

"I'm not paying into the Sunshine fund and paying for coffee! Thirty-five cents is outrageous."

He wasn't the only one who felt this way. At our next staff meeting, Reed had the new coffee system on the agenda, but his perspective wasn't what we expected.

"It's ridiculous," he was saying. "We install a very expensive, high-quality machine to bring you good coffee and you all can't even pay for it. I looked in the jar today and there was a lousy $5.95 and all of you have been drinking coffee for over a week."

"It's not about our unwillingness to pay," Frank piped up.

"We don't have change. It's hard to pay 35¢ when all you have is a dollar. We need a change jar."

"That's all it will take? A change jar?" Reed clarified.

Frank nodded.

The following morning Reed installed a change jar with $20 worth of quarters, dimes and nickels.

Lloyd and I were sipping hot coffee and eating our peanut butter sandwiches when Reed arrived to inspect the jar that afternoon. Fifteen cents rattled against the glass when he shook it.

"For crying out loud!" he bellowed, throwing his hands up in disgust. He whipped around ready to do battle with us just as he caught sight of our coffee thermoses from home. He looked down.

"Huston, your shoes are untied! Are you going to start tying your shoes or am I going to be yelling at you for the rest of my life?"

Operation Mayonnaise … what a trip down memory lane. To think all that happened over 50 years ago. Tonight my grandson is joining Lloyd and me and a few other fellas for poker. We get together every third Thursday of the month. We have a nickel ante, we eat meatloaf sandwiches, and all our shoelaces are untied.

◄ ▼ ►

Exploring Leaders' **Secrets**

Huston was a courageous follower. Sitting down to publicly eat lunch with Lloyd, despite all the slurs; confronting senior leadership about their lack of understanding regarding Lloyd's use of Cobalt; problem solving independently, despite the antiquated system; and befriending a man during an era of tremendous prejudice all demonstrate that while he was an imperfect follower, Huston was a follower that also chose to lead.

Like Huston, most of us are not in a position to say, "the buck stops here." In reality, the majority of us are straddling two roles: leader and follower. Business executives often report to boards or shareholders; politicians report to their party and constituents; executives of separate divisions still have parent companies to check in with; clergy have conferences or larger organizations as well as their parishioners to submit results to; and of course, any middle-manager or team captain must manage their direct reports while simultaneously managing-up in order to be successful in their own leadership role. Everyone has a boss.

Embracing the role of follower, while simultaneously leading, is not always easy. In fact, it can be downright frustrating. Working in a bureaucracy, needing to establish some sense of control over our work environment, and not always respecting the choices of upper management, are prevalent issues many of us deal with on a daily basis. Embracing the role of follower is even more difficult when we do not share our leaders' values, perceive our leaders as unworthy of their roles, or when the price of falling in line and demonstrating aligned servitude is too high.

Too often the myth, *"good, go-along followers will someday make for great leaders,"* is perpetuated by leaders who desire to keep their minions in check. Insecure leaders want their followers to be passive, but good followers are not passive—they are active. Active followers push boundaries, spot trends, share ideas, foster constructive dialogue, engage in healthy debate, and participate in problem solving so as to meet common goals and fulfill the mission of the organization. However, when active followers demonstrate their intellect and confidence, they can sometimes get cut off at the knees by insecure superiors who are threatened by their abilities to perform and lead. Insecure, unskilled leadership can turn harmless situations into unnecessary nightmares and benign environments into dangerous ones.

In the end, Huston's shoelace response to his boss was a passive-aggressive stance, but it did not start off that way. Keeping his laces untied was merely a personal choice for comfort. But human beings crave a sense of control. When untied laces became one of the few ways for Huston to exert control over his environment and demonstrate his personal freedom, they came to symbolize his resentment toward authority and his defiance of inept leadership.

Individuals in frustrating follower situations will feel like finding a different job. Indeed, leaving might be the ultimate action, but in tough times or extenuating circumstances, walking away is not always an option. Huston's story takes place in an era when workers didn't leap from company to company every few years, and when workplace cultures had a zero tolerance policy for challenging authority. Today's business culture gives followers more of a platform for questioning and challenging leaders, and those leaders who welcome active followers reap the benefits. Leaders who invite robust dialogue, encourage healthy debate and seek the input of diverse perspectives from their followers often gain greater commitment and buy-in from them.

While there are numerous examples of leadership decisions being made by *those-who-have* for *those-who-do-not*, thus placing empathy under assault and making common sense pretty rare, there are still times when followers must fall in line. For example, serving in the armed forces requires *unity of command* because lives depend on it. And there are times when leadership is not inept at all, but the follower is too rogue for the health of the culture or the good of the organization, and these individuals must find opportunities elsewhere. And then there are times when rogue followers demonstrate their convictions, help other followers to do the same, and thus become leaders of change.

"Bureaucracy is the epoxy that greases the wheels of progress."

–JAMES BOREN, Humorist

. . .

"Prisoners run the prison. Guards just carry the guns."

–ANONYMOUS

CONCEPTS

- Standing up for what's right
- Challenging the bureaucracy
- Creating personal space for leadership
- Taking initiative
- Establishing ownership
- Acting with courage

REFLECTING ON YOURS

1. When you believe in the cause, but not the leaders, how do you follow?

2. Who runs your organization, the "prisoners" or the "guards"?

3. Who of your supervisors have been bosses or bullies instead of leaders?

4. In your role as a follower, how do you help your leaders use their power effectively?

5. In your role as a leader, are you part of the problem or part of the solution?

6. How courageous are you in leading change?

◂ ▴ ▸

"I always wondered why somebody doesn't do something about that. Then I realized I was somebody."

—LILY TOMLIN, Actress & Comedian

BOBBIE MAE

FORMER POLITICAL CANDIDATE

GETTIN' REAL

EXECUTIVE WOMEN Magazine Feature Interview

EW: Last winter you were known as Bobbie Mae, the "get 'er dun Mayor" of Chokoloskee. You were running for Governor of the great state of Florida and affectionately referred to as a *Southern Charmer*. Today, you're Barbara Hashim, political poison for the Party. Yet in some ways you're more revered today than ever. What happened?

Bobbie Mae: On a rainy Thursday morning in early February I was addressing a small group of Floridians outside of Tampa; business leaders and students, five hundred, maybe six. By Thursday night I was a *Tampa Tribune* headline with a photo of me, barefoot, holding my boobs. But I'm getting ahead of myself.

EW: Back up then! We want the scoop.

Bobbie Mae: As you know, The *Leadership Federation League of Lakeland* invited me to kick off their annual Winter Conference. As a candidate with a strong—okay, a moderately strong political background—I needed these types of events to galvanize my image. I was a former mayor, and my political accomplishments consisted of a few of my signatures approving local city initiatives. But I was scrappy, making traction, and trying my best to stretch every campaign budget dollar as far as it would go. Everyone knew my stance on infrastructure, and it was no secret that I was running into a lot of opposition, so I tried to let the tension out a bit with some humor. I was trying to keep it light so to speak, so 20 seconds into my speech, I delivered my first joke:

> *I look forward to serving y'all through good times and*
> *bad. Just like a perfect political marriage! You know—*
> *stuck in it together, but sleeping in separate beds.*

That's when the booing started.

EW: Booing you?

Bobbie Mae: Yes. At first I thought they were booing the joke, but the booing turned into chanting, the chanting into yells, the yells demanding me to "get real or go home." Getting real—as in they wanted me to fully support *their* agenda, not my own. And I can't. I'm tired of ignoring the real issues just because some political organization has the ability to buy attention and votes for its own gain. It's morally repugnant. Something in me just snapped. Bobbie Mae, former beauty pageant winner and current political puppet was gone. I walked out from behind the podium and the well rehearsed script, stood before those boo-ers and decided to do battle as only I knew how. I told the truth.

My name is Barbara Hashim. I am 46 years old. Born in Houston, spent one year in Montgomery, Alabama, grew up in Berkeley, moved to Atlanta when I was 21. And I despise heels.

I kicked my shoes off, a little harder than I'd intended, one went flying.

Get real? Oh I can be quite real. And how did I get here?

Maybe it's the ridiculous levels of dysfunction in politics. Maybe it's all the snarky commentary with no real solutions, maybe it's all the reality TV making it harder for smarter, saner people to be heard. Maybe it was the astronomy professor I sat next to on the plane. I was writing a motivational speech on our country's leadership. He was full of contempt. Told me, "You politicians make things too complicated. My motto? 'Lead, follow or get out of the way.' That's all we need to know."

I nodded back to him. "I absolutely understand what you mean, Sir. It's just like you astronomy professors making things too complicated. I mean all we need to know is, Twinkle, twinkle little star."

EW: You were annoyed by his condescension?

Bobbie Mae: I was annoyed with it all. The whole chain of events. Leadership is not simple. Compared to political leadership—astronomy is a breeze. The star was there last night, it's going to be there tonight, and if you can't see it, move to where there's less light.

But back to the *League*—my blood was boiling, I could feel the sweat under my blouse, but for some reason I could not stop. I could not shut up. I was on a roll:

We are dumbing down the conversations and distracting leaders from the real issues.

Hillary gets a haircut and all of a sudden she "looks" presidential. Boehner cries and they question his manhood. Kim K has a $200 million app, Miley twerks to 20 million likes. What do all these things have in common? They don't matter! It's all noise. I have ideas. You have ideas. We have solutions. But too many of our leaders, too many of us, are talking about the noise rather than the issues that matter.

How did I get here, like this? It seemed like the only way to get people's attention was to glitz it up, sex it up, throw soundbites at you, keep up the glam—all the while trying to share a message that matters, and ultimately, hopefully, get something good done.

Instead, I got booed.

No one really started listening until I highlighted my hair, nicknamed myself Bobbie Mae, got a little support ... and "boom shake shake" shaked the room one night at a gala event. Hashtag Chokoloskee gala, hashtag boom shake, shake, shake the room, hashtag Bobbie Mae!

EW: And that was when you grabbed your chest?

Bobbie Mae: That was when I grabbed my campaign-encouraged-but-personally-financed breasts with both hands. I know, I know, but I did. And now two million people have thumbs-up'd this clip.

EW: And as you often say, "Now here we are ... getting real." Slightly ironic wouldn't you say?

Bobbie Mae: The boob thing, it's complicated. Crazy really.

EW: What started all this craziness? What got you into politics?

Bobbie Mae: Religion. I found myself praying for patience ... every day. Sooo many people sidetracked by the wrong stuff. So many people looking to blame someone rather than solve something. I got in that trap for a while too. When you're cynical it's easy to sound smart, to appear above it all, but it's the optimist who sees the future. It's the optimist who creates a solution where the cynics cannot.

Life is a crazy journey. We're all fractions of ourselves, pretending to be whole, and it's too easy to be passive. We walk around with passive judgments all day long: my boss didn't make the goals clear; my company doesn't do meaningful work; my spouse doesn't understand me. But this rationale attempts to make everyone else responsible.

When do we start asking ourselves, how do I get clarity on my goals? How do I create meaning? How do I build a better relationship? That's what I was asking myself ... when do I stand up to make a difference instead of just pouring a glass of wine and complaining at a cocktail party?! When do politicians stop trying to please everybody and start saying the things we need to hear? Maybe I should have been a preacher. No one boos a preacher for telling the truth.

EW: What do you mean when you talk about being a part of the noise versus rising above the noise?

Bobbie Mae: If we want to set the stage for a better future, we must be better leaders of ourselves. Physician heal thyself, you know? We have to know who we really are, what we really stand for, and we need to be very clear on our story versus the story that everyone else wants to write about us.

We must be so clear on what we're aiming for we can see it a mile away. We can look past the noise; we can pay attention to what matters.

Our country is hungry for meaningful hope and change ... and looking for someone else to deliver. Tolstoy once said, *"Everybody thinks of changing humanity and nobody thinks of changing himself."*

It starts with me ... getting more real. It starts with you getting more real. More clear, more curious, more engaged, more honest, more thoughtful, more understanding. Asking ourselves, "Did I do my best to be real today? Did I do my best to pay attention to what matters?"

EW: Is it really that straightforward?

Bobbie Mae: It's simple, not simplistic. My friend Maureen believes the reason there are so few female politicians is that it's too much trouble putting make-up on two faces. I will not be two-faced. I will pay attention to what matters.

EW: So why should our readers vote for you … if you choose to get back in the race?

Bobbie Mae: That was my last speech as a political candidate. As citizens of this great nation, we crave truth, but sadly, our partisan system doesn't encourage nor support it. The only way to change our politicians is to change the way we vote.

EW: So no more politics, ever?

Bobbie Mae: What do you say to someone when they tell you that you can be photographed Christmas shopping, but not eating Jesus' birthday cake. When your own Party says you want to appear American, but not to come across as a Bible thumper. That you need to get your boobs done or the men won't pay attention to what you're saying. Hello?! Clearly these men are not interested in my *words.*

What do you do when you want to have a real dialogue about unions, wages, potholes, or civil rights and they are more concerned you will say what you like to eat or don't like to eat and an entire industry will be offended and sue you?

I said on live television one night, *I don't like kale,* and they all just about wet their big boy pants.

What do you say when they start telling you that you can't kiss babies anymore?

EW: You can't kiss babies?!

Bobbie Mae: Not unless they're under a year. Wait, it might be nine months now. Anyway, it got crazy. I enhanced my body, I stretched my politics, I shunned my beliefs, I sat on the fence, I talked out both sides of my mouth, and for what? There are serious issues, issues that need challenging, issues that need knocking over, and I think there might be better ways to solve them than politics.

EW: You sound defeated.

Bobbie Mae: I sound smarter. I have not given up. I'm simply choosing to take my energy and apply it where I can measure the difference in something other than campaign dollars, party votes and Internet *Likes*. Yes, some days I wonder if I hadn't snapped in front of an audience would I have run the course and made a bigger difference, or would the system have eaten me up and spit me out anyway? And days like today, when I get excited that in a few years the interview will be about the problems my political action group solved, and *not* my Internet video that got more *Likes* than that cute kitten that made it out of the garbage truck unharmed.

EW: So just to be clear, no more politics?

Bobbie Mae: Never say never, but I'm pretty sure my politicking days are done. I mean, once you've lost respect because you've given away all of yourself, how do you get it back?

EW: Respect or the pieces of yourself you gave away?

Bobbie Mae: Both. I want to be a "get real" leader. This is me. Making a difference in meaningful ways. The real me. One-hundred percent authentic Barbara Mary Hashim. One-hundred percent.

EW: Except for your chest.

Bobbie Mae: Well, then … 98 percent!

Editor's note: The day we went to print, the "Kitty is the Litter" video surpassed Ms. Bobbie Mae Hashim's "boom shake shake" video by 22 million views.

◄ ▼ ►

Exploring Leaders' **Secrets**

When Bobbie Mae played the role of political chameleon, she placed herself in a precarious position of compromising her views and her understanding of various issues. She ended up talking out of both sides of her mouth and making statements she later regretted. When we ignore our personal views for some external gain, (gains such as campaign donations, votes, capital investors, volunteers, stock prices, or publicity), we may gain a short-term objective, but we ultimately lose our authentic voice and diminish our results. Ignoring our understanding of issues and silencing our voice, can lead to hazy values, dodgy decisions, unprincipled actions, and a lot of finger pointing when things go sideways.

Social media bombards us with messages about what we should think, believe, say, and do. The Internet is constantly expanding the breadth and depth of this input, and the noise can be overwhelming. This noise is often static and distracting. We must filter it for the sake of our identity and for the sake of our mission. Filtering out the noise allows us to separate what we think from what we are told to think. Adhering to our inner voice is what gives us our ability to filter the noise—to separate the wheat from the chaff.

These cynical "noisy" messages frequently focus on what's not working. They emphasize dysfunction, perpetuate negative discourse and rarely include viable solutions. It's much easier to criticize others actions and ideas than it is to offer up viable solutions. These "static" messages incite little forward action, thus perpetuating the mediocrity they protest.

When Bobbie Mae returned to expressing her understanding of the issues, she got real, real fast. Living boldly requires a stronger, more energetic voice than the lazier voice used to criticize, cast blame, avoid accountability, perpetuate problems, please pundits or appease supporters. When we tune into the few channels we deem worthy, while simultaneously creating a much stronger frequency for our own solution-oriented voice, we rally followers who will help us create real change.

There is a double bonus that accrues when we take a stand and speak up passionately and authentically for our views. First, we earn committed and passionate followers who take action and help us. Second, these dedicated loyal followers often receive a bonus from us in return because we give them the courage to voice their views.

"It takes nothing to join the crowd. It takes everything to stand alone."

–HANS F. HANSEN

. . .

"For what shall it profit a man, if he shall gain the whole world, and lose his own soul?"

–MARK 8:36

CONCEPTS

- Chameleon effect—striving to be please everybody
- Acquiescing to others' demands to further our own gain
- Blaming others
- Optimist or cynic
- Losing our voice
- Tuning out the noise
- Speaking our truth—getting real

REFLECTING ON YOURS

1. When have you lied, white lied or "gone along" for personal gain?

2. When have you kept quiet when you should have spoken up?

3. Are you more of a cynic or an optimist? Is that glass half full, half empty, or just too big?!

4. What rhetoric/noise currently distracts you from your purpose and passion?

5. If you ran for political office, what would be the first plank in your platform?

6. If you got "more real," who in your life might "abandon" you and who might "embrace" you even more?

◀▲▶

"What you do speaks so loudly that I cannot hear what you say."

—RALPH WALDO EMERSON

MAC

CEO

Lookin' in
the Mirror

I drink seven to nine vodkas a night. To be fair, I mix it with Sprite Zero. It's the 96 calories that nutritionists say I can walk off in 27 minutes that makes me chuckle. The only walking after nine vodkas will be to the waiting driver when I'm ready to go home. I'm a big guy. 6'6". I carry my weight well. Most people, when they meet me, don't think I'm fat. They just see a big guy. I'm robust. My doctor says I have great cholesterol levels. Nothing to worry about.

My favorite restaurant is on the corner of Van Dyke and Third. Bones. Third generation steakhouse. I like mine well done. I know, people say they'll give you the worst cut when you ask for it well done, but these are my guys, they're like family. They know to keep my glass full, my vodka cold, they never have to give me a menu and I never have to send my steak back. Mondays, Tuesdays and Wednesdays my waiter is Danny. Thursdays it's Tommy or his wife Jean. I try not to eat out on Friday and Saturday. Family time. I want to be home with Bonnie and the kids. Our oldest, Eric, usually has a football game on Friday nights anyway. Sunday is for God. We eat at home, as a family, a big dinner that Bonnie fixes.

I've got life by the tail. Life is a choice, you know. I choose the right side, the bright side. I do not wallow in misery, I do not make nor accept excuses, I do not let the world pull the wool over my eyes. I choose to be a force for positivity. A force!

Take for instance the moron that blocked the lane the other night. I had spent the day at a double header. Love baseball. One of the finest sports invented by God, definitely not Doubleday. Had an SUV full of my sales guys. We'd had a fine day, ending on a win, and then we were stuck in horrible stadium traffic. We'd even waited in the Club afterwards, enjoying a few more rounds, finishing the last of the cheesecake, but now ... we were blocked by a woman who was trying to cross on-coming traffic. She had stopped in my lane. Total blockage. Three lanes going north and she wanted to cross all three to pull into the gas station to my right. Clue-free. That's what I call these individuals that want to go against the flow.

"Don't make me a part of your mistake," I called out, causing some of the guys to chuckle. This is one of my mottos. Just because you screw up doesn't mean it needs to be *my* screw up. She didn't move, just gestured like a turtle caught on her back. There was another guy driving behind her. Her fender was crumbled, his fender was pushed into a V-shape, they'd clearly been in a little dust-up, but crossing in front of me, blocking me, while the other two lanes moved by was pretty annoying. I wanted to get out of there. I was done. The day was over. Time to go home and go to bed. But no, it was not to be. Ms. Incompetent and Inconsiderate could not see that she had made an idiotic choice. I leaned on the horn. "Get out of the way!" I roared. "You can't turn here! Back up! Back up before I hit you myself!"

Finally, and it was by no means fast nor efficient, drivers in the other two lanes heard my horn and yelling, realized what was going on, and stopped to let these two fools pass through to the other side. By then I swear we'd lost ten minutes. Maybe twenty. I was so pissed. But did I let her foolish choices stay with me? No. Absolutely not. Every day is a choice. I choose to be the captain of my own ship. I whistled the rest of the way home. You cannot let the clue-free chart the course of your day.

Now don't get me wrong, I've faced my share of troubles. Bonnie wanted a divorce eight years ago. Never, I said. We took vows. I whistle through. It's a choice. We have three kids now, Eric, Blaine and Daniel. We lost a baby girl at three days old, but God wanted her for Himself. I truly believe He needed her more. Obviously, He did. Bonnie has different opinions about these things. They don't serve her well. She suffers from bouts of depression.

Most families have swear jars. We have a sad jar. I set it up, told Bonnie that every time I saw her looking sad I'd toss a quarter in the jar. Filled up immediately. Ping. Ping. Ping. I kept tossing them in. And instead of choosing happiness you know what she did. She drove straight to the bank, came back with a $100 bill, stuffed it in the jar, and said, "Save your quarters, Mac." I keep telling her it's a choice, and I believe one day she will wake up and see that I'm right.

My employees know that I'm right. I have been voted best CEO in the state three years in a row. I am humbled, truly I am. It's a privilege to serve. I am not one of these guys that will tell you I followed my passion. No, Siree, I do it for the money. I'm a straight shooter. I have grown this company 24% each year for the last six years in a row, and why? Because money is a tool. That's all it is. Don't give it any more power than it deserves. It simply gives me the ability to do some good in this world.

Good that others simply don't get. I've lost six supervisors in the last two years. Blessing in disguise. My critics say 24%

growth was weak, that if we'd been paying better attention we could have leveraged market opportunities. I say that not every opportunity is a good one. I hear them out and then I ask them to step in line. If they can't step in line, I ask 'em to step out. The Board is grumbling that we're having trouble keeping top talent, but they're not top talent if they can't see my vision. I help those who help me.

When people ask me what I do for a living I do not say that I am a CEO or that I run a $200 million manufacturing plant. No. At the end of the day I'm a Dream Director. It's not as touchy-feely as it sounds. It's what I do, why I wake up in the morning. My Chief Operating Officer has four kids who need an education and he likes boats. Big boats. My Human Resources Manager has twins who need braces and an aging mother who needs round-the-clock care. That's why I get up in the morning. I just happen to manufacture parts.

I've won best CEO three years running because my employees know I have their backs. You give me 100%, I'll give you back 110%. I don't put up with mediocrity. You have the team you deserve. Most CEOs don't want to hear this because their teams are mediocre at best. But what you settle for in life is a reflection of you. What are you willing to accept? Let me tell you: the lowest common denominator you accept says far more about you than it does that underachiever. I only tolerate managers who are smart enough to follow my lead. Don't get me wrong, give somebody a chance, help them help themselves, but when I want success for someone more than they want it for themselves, I wash my hands of them because they will not bring me down. No, Siree.

I attended a nation-wide conference in Los Angeles last week on leadership. Not exactly what I was hoping for, but there were a few nuggets of wisdom. Only one real innovative speaker … the rest were a bunch of run-of-the-mill motivational types, nothing new, nothing fresh, shouting out trite rhymes such as, *We can't heal what we refuse to reveal.* A bunch of emotional Dr. Seuss-es.

I sat at a table with other business owners who were whining about their employees. This drives me crazy. How can you be whining and leading? It's an oxymoron. One CEO was complaining that he has to do all the thinking. Arrogant and annoying. And I said so. He was miffed, but I told him I wasn't being a jerk, that he just sounded arrogant. I told him he should ask more questions in meetings. Start posing bigger, better, bolder questions and see what his people had to say. Hell, I run meetings with agendas composed only of questions. I should be doing the least amount of talking in any given meeting. He might try it. But I'd put money on the fact that he goes back to the office and starts doing exactly what he did yesterday.

Some so-called leaders drive you crazy. It's been said that you can lead a horse to water but you can't make him drink. True enough, but a leader can make him thirsty. That's my job. Make him feel so parched, so excited to take that first sip, he drinks the whole damn gallon and thinks it was his brilliant idea.

I have my own business ideas, but I still like hearing what my employees have to say. Makes it easier in getting them to drink down the line. Also helps me make better decisions in the long run. They may be sheep, but if the shepherd is not aware of what's going on in the flock he cannot control them. And there's usually one or two really bright ones, and if you pay attention, really talk to those sheep, they'll make you a better shepherd.

Where I don't need input is my personal life. I know right from wrong. I know what sin is. I don't need some activist trying to tell me that the world is changing. Of course it is. I use my iPad almost every day now to keep up with the stock market and my baseball stats, but fundamentally things haven't changed. The truth is the truth, and I'm tired of this generation, or some new age do-gooder telling me we are all one energy, that family dynamics are changing or that couples therapy is okay. I do not need to get in touch with my feelings. I know exactly how I feel. I feel like it's all horse manure.

Bonnie, the kids and I disagree here too, so touchy-feely conversations are now avoided at our dining room table. I have zero tolerance … but if I really can't get out of it, then just refill my glass. Last Sunday, Eric shared that Tracy Benton, the high school's wide receiver, is in therapy. And I do not mean physical. What's this world coming to? Football players in therapy? If he were my kid I'd tell him to suck it up and move forward.

I chewed my meat slowly when Eric told me about his teammate. My first thought, *You named your son, Tracy. What did you expect?* My second thought, *Every day is a choice. This boy needs to choose to get his own head screwed on straight.* But did I say anything? Nope. I was not going to let this conversation ruin my Sunday dinner. I stood up, walked to the liquor cabinet and started whistling.

◂ ▾ ▸

Exploring Leaders' **Secrets**

When we hear the word "blind spot," many people conjure up an image of driving down the highway unable to see the car tucked just out of sight from either the rearview or side view mirrors. On the road, the sound of a horn, or the appearance of the hidden car at the last second can prevent a collision. Sometimes, unfortunately, that car remains in our blind spot right up until impact.

The same is true when it comes to our own blind spots; our weaknesses and vulnerabilities exist … but just out of view, even when we look in the mirror. Occasionally, they honk at us, and we catch a glimpse of our own limitations, fallacies, false stories, limiting beliefs and/or bad behaviors in the mirror and we adjust, safely enhancing our driving skills along the way. Other times we have scarier near-misses or even a fender-bender. Sometimes, tragically, we are oblivious to the fact that the five-car-pile-up we hear about on the news later was instigated by our own poor actions, or we find ourselves in the middle of that pile-up.

Mac's ability to filter events in his favor supports his superior self-righteousness on the surface, but his drinking reveals that he may indeed be aware that his "style of driving" is causing pain in others and ultimately within himself. However, like many leaders with blind spots in a confined part of their lives, it's hard for Mac to correct his driving at home when at work he is often rewarded for his ability to be in the right gear at the right time.

Part of the difficulty of seeing our blind spots is because they hide behind our strengths.

- Are you so optimistic that you wait too long to deal with the reality of a failing project?

- Are you so positive that you dismiss other's real pain thus causing more of it?

- Are you so good at analyzing the data that you forget to message it in a compelling way?

- Are you such an expert in your field that you forget to check the latest findings?

- Are you so focused on being right that you lose sight of what's wrong with your behavior?

- Are you so indoctrinated in a view that you shut down understanding of another's because it seems threatening rather than informative?

Blind spots can weaken our effectiveness, diminish results, and create harmful unintended consequences. Blind spots exist in part because we are wired to see ourselves favorably. We have insider knowledge about our intentions. When we make a mistake, we can explain our good intentions—even if only to ourselves. Sometimes our explanation is candidly honest and other times we fabricate a filter to make our objective more pure, more justified—again, if only to ourselves.

With others, we see their actions, but we do not have access to the intentions behind their behaviors. Without access to their intentions, we make assumptions to explain their behavior, and what we make up often supports our own interpretation, not their intent. These false filters and interpretations can lead to self-justification, which frequently leads to self-righteousness. Assumptions about others' intentions as well as our own, falsely perceived as correct, become truthfully dishonest for us and they obstruct our view. We see events through the lens of validation and confirmation rather than revocation and contradiction. Over time we become less open to hearing contrary points of view and are less tolerant of back seat drivers who may indeed be providing constructive feedback that can improve our ability to drive safely.

While it is indeed difficult to see our own blind spots because, um, well, we're blind to them, the bad news is that others see them vividly. However, bad news can be good news. When we change lanes while driving 65 mph, it's obvious that we need to check our blind spot. When we're changing a fast moving organization, or getting ready to make a bold decision in our personal lives it is safer to allow, or better yet ask, someone to point out the cars we can't see. Not just anyone, but someone that we trust to do so in a supportive, caring way—someone we will not punish for saying yes to our request for being our back-seat-driver.

The irony of self-righteousness is that when we discover some of our own fallacies, shortcomings, or blind spots and correct them, we will feel even better about our amazing virtue and driving skills.

Caution … while we're yelling at the guy in front of us for not using his signal, just remember, we still may not see that gray car hanging back … just out of sight.

"Not for the first time in my life, and certainly not for the last, a self-righteous gloom had edged out all semblance of logic."

–NICK HORNBY, *Fever Pitch*

• • •

"Make no judgments where you have no compassion."

–ANNE MCCAFFREY, Novelist

CONCEPTS

- Ignoring or failing to see our blind spots
- Possessing limited or false awareness about our own strengths and weaknesses
- Unconsciously biased or prejudiced
- Self-righteousness
- Unhealthy coping strategies
- Seeing others' blind spots through a lens of judgment instead of compassion

REFLECTING ON YOURS

1. What behaviors and traits differentiate good bosses from good leaders?

2. Who is your welcomed back-seat driver?

3. When you look in the mirror, do you like what you see, both at home and at work?

4. How do you help others see their blind spots? Who are you a back-seat driver for?

5. What constructive feedback from others has helped you be more aware of your own blind spots?

◄ ▲ ►

"No one saves us but ourselves. No one can and no one may. We ourselves must walk the path."

—BUDDHA

DEENA

STAYIN' ON
YOUR PATH

I LOST IT EXACTLY 9 days, 12 hours and 17 minutes ago. Total. Rage. Meltdown.

My creative team staged an intervention. Rage-us-interruptus. It was embarrassing. Mortifying, really. But okay, sorta funny and slightly pathetic. Maybe more than slightly.

They called me into our conference room and sat me down. Allie gently removed my Bluetooth from my ear while Katie wiped away the mascara streaking down my cheek. Charlie closed the lid to my laptop. "No more Internet," they said. "You're going on the wagon for two weeks."

All right—I'll admit it—utterly pathetic.

Earlier that day, we were brainstorming promotional ideas for our new product when we surfed our way into a competitor, a woman who used to be an old friend. Her new website was up. It was slick and cool, and I felt like she beat me to the punch. We were in the middle of redesigning our site, but hers was already up, looking good and making me question why I always seem to be five steps behind everyone else. I took a deep breath and mentally recited a positive affirmation: *Her path is not my path.* I repeated it again, *Her path is not my path.* I could still feel my chest tightening so I thought to myself, *Our website will rock in a few months. Our website will rock in a few months.* I felt my neck muscles clench. *Her site's amazing and up! It's already up! She beat you. She beat you. She beat you, you stupid moron. She beat you!*

Our website is months away from launching, with a developer telling me he might need even more time. I looked at my team and realized I was under a microscope of stares. I dug my fingernails into my palm, smiled my full-watt fake smile and said, "Good for her! Okay, who wants Chinese?!"

What's wrong with me?! I read all the books on abundance. I keep a gratitude journal. I want all my friends to be wildly successful, and the minute—no—the second I see somebody else successfully kickin' it in my space I lose it. I seethe with competitive jealousy: it's not me getting to wave at my ship as it comes in! Where the heck is my ship?! Was it lost at sea? Or is it one of those cruise lines where everyone gets food poisoning from the shrimp buffet? I picture my sluggish web-designer—is he the one who didn't keep the shrimp properly refrigerated? Did he not wash his hands after using the restroom? Are there NOT signs on my cruise-ship that say "Employees Must Wash Hands?!"

After a lunch of Kung Pao spite, I was back in my office racing through emails—237 to be exact—of which at least sixty plus were eblasts promising to help me become more efficient—when I came upon the subject line, "Green with Envy?"

It was from an executive life coach who was always hocking her nine-week online program. What timing! I clicked play.

Turns out this coach had a jealous moment when her famous friend was having a success—something about a celebrity chef agreeing to cater the friend's party. But it was okay, because this executive life coach turned her frown upside down and realized that a rising tide lifts all rafts ... and then she skipped back to her gated community and consulted with the pool-boy about pH levels, and ... oh, for crying out loud! You skinny, wealthy, beautiful, get-rich-quick-social-media-can't-keep-a-job-so-now-I'll-coach whore. Yep, you heard me, you webinar-twittering e-wench.

What's with these social media folks selling their social media savvy? Where did these people come from? They pop up like bunnies and it's like they have instant success. It's maddening! The Internet is like one huge, digital, infomercial bacchanalia for get-rich-quick schemes and the only people getting rich are the ones selling their social-media-mass-marketing expertise to every other entrepreneur out there.

The week prior, in a moment of weakness, I signed up for a webinar that was "sure to knock my socks off," complete with rave reviews from prior webinar participants and testimonials galore so I thought ... *Why not? It's only $79.*

This webinar host ... this marketing guru ... this thought-leader extraordinaire ... couldn't get his PowerPoint to work. The conference center's projector had problems, he claimed, laughing it off and promising that slides or no slides, his content would be so incredibly good we wouldn't care and he'd email us all the deck later anyway. Then he proceeded to share with us that the very best thing we could do to be highly successful entrepreneurs was to schedule more *me* time. "Take off a week, take off a month. No one works in August anyway," he continued, and I just realized I had paid $79 to have a man tell me I could be rich if I'd take more time off.

Don't get me wrong, I totally believe in getting away from it all and going to the beach and reading *Fifty Shades* of anything, but I did not just pay 79 bucks to have some podcast-douche tell me that the secret to my marketing success and overall business wealth is lounging around in August when I have a team of people that would greatly appreciate my ability to make payroll.

I am a high functioning fake-it-till-you-make-it-go-getter

of an entrepreneur who just celebrated seven years in business ... and I am experiencing the itch. Not the itch of jumping ship and having an affair with a new company ... just the seven year itch of *What does it take?! Why aren't I more successful by now?* I'm busting my butt. I have been putting in sixty-plus hour weeks for the past seven years despite the fact that everywhere I turn some coach is harping in my ear, "Are you working hard or are you working smart?" What I want to say is, "That is not a helpful question! And you're not the first person to ask it!" And then maybe I would smack them with a copy of their book. But instead I just smile, high wattage, and say, "I can't afford to hire any more team members, so right now I think I'm working hard and smart."

But I am barely making payroll, barely keeping my head afloat, and my overhead is staggering no matter how much I trim costs. I pop antacids like they are candy, and I leave way too much hair on my brush every morning from stress. But of course, my competitor, the one with the fabulous new website, great hair! Gobs of it! Maddening!! I work and I work and I work—but no matter what I do I fall short.

And occasionally when we do get a win, it seems more like a slap in the face because it's a mini-win, not a huge win. My ship comes in—but it's just a tiny sail-boat with rips in the faux-leather seats. It smells like fish. It's just enough of a win to keep the treadmill going. Just enough for me to leave the binoculars around my neck, to scan the horizon for that bigger ship that must be out there somewhere.

But it never is.

So nine days ago, it happened. Charlie slipped his iPad onto my desk and said, *"Read."* I could tell by his tone that this was not going to be a joyous moment.

And there she was: beautiful, full head of hair, smiling, looking amazingly like the Cheshire cat. The headline: *Millionaire Entrepreneur Shares Her Secret Sauce.*

I scanned the article, my blood pressure rising, my eyeballs bulging and every cell in my body wanting to scream, "IT'S NOT FAIR!" But even to me that sounded immature—lame, in fact—so instead, with one grand sweeping gesture, I swiped everything off my desk. Papers and pens went flying, along with my coffee cup and the crystal *Entrepreneur of the Year* award and my *Thirty Under Thirty* award I'd garnered seven years before. Charlie's iPad cracked with a shattering sound of doomed fate when it hit the wall, and I actually looked at the mess I created for one full beat before I howled.

Yes, I howled. A gut-wrenching, coyote's lost its mate, *Adam-Levine's-pipes-have-got-nothing-on-me* kind of howl.

I said things I can't repeat. You'll just have to trust me—it was foul-mouthed poetry like I've never produced before. I cussed until I had no breath left in me. I cussed until I felt like the walls might need to be repainted. Somewhere in that tirade Charlie was smart enough to duck out.

I had been stone silent for about three minutes when Allie walked in with a bottle of vodka and two shot glasses left from the holiday party and filled one for me. But it was too late for that—I was already moving from rage to numb all by myself. I didn't want to add stupid to the list as well.

"How do they do it?! That's what I want to know. HOW DO THEY DO IT?! Where do they find the time? Who do they know?! What do they do to get there? I'd say they have money, family connections, friends in the right places, and some of them do, but not all of them. Is it just a lucky break that gets luckier? Is it just that I have no clue what I'm doing? Am I not smart enough? Not savvy enough? Not good enough? Not worthy enough?"

I didn't want to say it out loud, even to Allie: *Am I just a poser?*

I gingerly stepped through the broken crystal, bent down and picked up the iPad, and looked at the entrepreneur's smiling face behind the crack. I looked up at Allie who was having no problem drinking the vodka she'd poured for me.

"Why can't I be happy for her?"

Allie looked dumbfounded. "She's your arch rival who stabbed you in the back and took your three best clients."

"She was my roommate all through college … Who chose money over friendship … And I'm secretly enraged about her and everyoe else's success!"

"Well, it's not so secret now," Allie said, pointing to the onlookers. I looked up and just as I did the entire team ducked their heads and scattered. The escapee-from-the-asylum spectacle was over.

"She met Oprah," I said.

Allie nodded.

"There's a picture of her here with Bradley Cooper. Is THAT the 'Secret Sauce'?"

"It doesn't matter," Allie replied, pouring another shot. "Here, seriously … even just one sip. You need it."

I looked at Allie. I picked up the iPad again. Smiled.

"You mind?"

Allie nodded: "Go ahead."

And I flung it. Hard. I watched it hit the wall, and smack to the floor. I took three deep breaths. And I erupted.

"FOR THE LOVE OF GOD WHAT DOES IT TAKE?! TELL ME! How does anyone in this world figure this thing out?!"

Allie looked at me and nodded understandingly.

"May I?" she asked, holding her shot-glass over her head.

I nodded. Allie slammed her shot-glass to the floor. It bounced and hit her in the shin. She yelped, and we both burst out laughing. Mine turned to tears, but mostly it was glorious to get it out. Alcohol was not the release I needed.

Allie was kind enough to give me a few moments alone before my team quietly showed up at the door, with the look of intervention in their eyes.

That was 9 days, 12 hours and 3 minutes ago. A lifetime. My staff didn't hold me to Internet-cold-turkey for more than about a day, of course, after I'd made an enormous show of apology. Top-notch sushi was brought in—twice—and over some amazing yellowtail we laughed it off like the whole episode never happened. Well, some of them laughed it off. Four of them found new jobs—including Charlie.

For nine days now I can see it clearly: I'm drowning. Drowning in competitive bull, drowning in the rat race, drowning in the fight to get to the top.

No. No, that's not right—I'm drowning in insecurity. That's what it is. Drowning in my sense of inadequacy, in my loss of confidence, in my loss of leadership. Somewhere along the way I became just another boss … and not a very well-behaving one. And I've become a jealous follower, more focused on those that I despise instead of carving out my own path.

Where did the *me* that set up this company to begin with go? I liked that person. I used to laugh, I used to be funny. I used to be spontaneous and playful and creative. Now I'm driven, angry, stale—a workaholic automaton. I'm so busy watching others on their paths, it's slowing me down on my own. I want my mojo back.

I need a second act.

◁ ▽ ▷

Exploring Leaders' **Secrets**

Are you drowning? Drowning in burnout, competitive malarkey, inadequacies, self-doubt and/or insecurity? Somewhere along the path to "success," leaders often drift onto someone else's path or into a ditch of desperation and self-destruction.

Juxtapose this drifting with our ego's simultaneous belief that we are worthy of a great deal more than the gopher-wheel-nonsense we wake up to everyday, and what we endure is a tremendous amount of stress, competitive anxiety and inner turmoil. The eye-opening, niggling truth that may haunt us, that may stare us down the barrel of a rifle, is that we don't feel secure in who we are, what we are doing or the road we are taking.

Looming failure can bring out the worst in our thinking and our behaviors. *Fast Company* magazine arrives and we find ourselves asking, *Why didn't I accomplish more by age 30?* We run into an old colleague and discover her kids are excelling in some international program, mastering two foreign languages and participating in global youth studies, and we ask, *Why can't my dog just come when I call her?!* We hear about someone's successes and instead of wishing them well, we go into our office, and like Deena, we rant and rage and throw things. We act like a temper-tantrum throwing child … we act like anything but a leader.

Sometimes we are lucky and a truth reveals itself before we lose our dignity. We think: *Because you are trying to make it the way everyone else is making it ... not the way you must uniquely choose to make it ... your efforts are stymied.*

When this elucidating truth surfaces it can be terrifying and relaxing. Terrifying because our own path may not be as good or as timely as someone else's (as judged by us) or relaxing, because maybe, for just this once, we can let go and see how things turn out without us forcing events to happen like they happen for someone else.

When leaders compare themselves to everything and everyone, they lose their power and ultimately their mojo. When their mojo is lost they hang onto failed situations too long and sometimes self-destruct. When leaders lose their sense of self, when they drift too far, they lose their followers.

Deena realizes she's reached the end of act one. It's time for her to change her response, devise a better game plan, and kick herself into gear if she wants to win the battle in act three. Reclaiming her mojo is vital to actualizing her true brilliance.

The world is going by so fast that too many leaders focus on just trying to hang on. That's the fallacy. We don't hang on, we let go. We let go of everybody's else's path and just go back to our own. The whole "fake it till you make it"—what if we're just faking it, and faking it some more, and then we fake ourselves right into believing the malarkey we created, and that's all we get—a life of malarkey—a life of walking the wrong path.

"Why do we feel jealousy? …
it's true that people who feel
inadequate, insecure, or overly
dependent tend to be more
jealous than others."

—HELEN FISHER

• • •

"Comparison is an act of violence
against the self."

—IYANLA VANZANT

CONCEPTS

- Walking our own path vs. drifting onto another's
- Losing our mojo
- Burnout and self-destruction
- Competitive jealousy
- Failing and recovering
- Rebuilding

REFLECTING ON YOURS

1. When has someone else's success tweaked you or caused a full-fledged fit of jealousy? At the time, what was lacking, crumbling or unfulfilled in your own life?

2. When have you strayed to someone else's path or simply stepped off your own? How did you find your way back?

3. What personal clues serve as warning signs that you might be nearing the edge of your resiliency?

4. Who and what are primary sources for fueling your energy and sparking your mojo today? Might you need new sources?

◄▲►

"Some of us think holding on makes us strong; but sometimes it is letting go."

–HERMAN HESSE

LYZA

CEO

Payin' the Price

Our current house has a double shower in the master bath. Mike insisted we buy a house with a double-headed shower. When we were shopping for the "rest of our lives" house 12 years ago he flirted with me about showering together, refusing to buy the one house that was perfect except for the missing "second head" in the master shower and the lack of a hot tub. I gave in, I thought, okay, this is important to him, and hello, he still finds me sexy. It seemed like a good compromise at the time. Why I didn't suggest we just install another head once we moved into the otherwise perfect house is eluding me now. Obviously, I wasn't thinking clearly, but rather, I was thinking through the fog of steamy shower doors.

I've asked him to join me in the shower so many … one time. We've made love in the shower exactly one time. The week we moved in. He avoids it. I asked him Tuesday if he'd like to get ready for work together, he said he had to get the recyclables out. *Go ahead, shower without me.* I asked him last Saturday. *Got to run to Home Depot and get new tanks for the grill.*

We make love in bed. Always in bed. Never in the pool, never on the lounge chair, not once on the chair made for two. In bed. We arrive showered and undressed. No slow teasing removal of lingerie, no let me unbutton that for you, nope. Crawl in, do it, and then he'll walk the house to make sure all the doors are locked and the security system is set. It's quite romantic. And we do it seasonally, whether he really wants to or not. The trumpet vine blooms and I get excited.

Where did this series of events begin? How did I end up with a double-headed shower and a husband that doesn't ever turn it on for me? We're not supposed to have regrets. Bad experiences and wrong choices are character building—to be perceived as learning opportunities. I'm not so sure this isn't self-help hooey.

Why is it so hard for some of us to say, *Hey, I did the best that I could at the time that I made that decision, but it still turned out to be a lousy decision, and I regret that I didn't know better, that I didn't get a crystal ball, because the outcome stinks.* Do-over. That's what I want. Can I have a do-over please? Because this isn't what I planned for my life. My life is a one-headed shower in a two-headed shower stall. This shouldn't be happening. But it is. It's reality. And every time I argue with reality I lose.

My daughter Janie came home for Thanksgiving break last week, and it was the first time that I was jealous of my daughter. Oh, there have been moments over the years when I wished for her line-free complexion or her skinny hips, but it was a silly craving to get my body back. She got her skinny hips from me, how rude of her not to give 'em back! But it was all good-natured and fun and amusing, until last week. At twenty she's just uncurling, just twirling into a series of incredible experiences that she will eventually call her life. And I looked at her, really looked at her and just for a second I wanted to be her. I've always said you couldn't pay me enough to go back in time, but just for a second I wanted it all ahead of me, I wanted a do-over.

It's tough when youth kicks you out of her club. I received my marching orders seven months ago. I immediately got Botox. Spent a month looking like I wanted to kill everybody in sight because Dr. Deborah didn't do the outside of my eyes to keep the brows even. They dipped down like a V-geese formation. Evil geese. I looked pissed off, but then one morning it smoothed out and I looked lovely. It's addicting. No more highway lines running across my forehead. Mike flipped out. *You're beautiful just the way you are. Why would you do this?*

Um … because I look younger, feel better and thought you might make love to me under a hot double-spray of water if I wasn't frowning all the time. And hey, when the geese's migration path returns I'll know it's our season.

It's unsettling when your heart and head do not align … and you must accept it. Most times we don't consent to the truth behind a misalignment. We simply rationalize both until there's a frontrunner. My gut tells me X, my head tells me Y and I'll settle for not making a decision for another week until a choice is obviously justified.

But tonight I'm very clear that misalignment is the alignment of this situation. Crooked is as straight as it's going to get. Crooked must be accepted because crooked is the truth, and there's no way to unbend the fact that warped is where we're at, and warped still requires a decision.

How do you know when "out" is the best decision? That "out" isn't a cop-out it's just "out" and better. Out has never been an option. We always said we believed in our vows. It's been a long time since we said we believed in us, or one another, just our vows. I'm not sure what this means, but I don't want to be a quitter. I can't be perceived as a quitter. If my employees knew how messed up my marriage was they would smirk. Some of them would be like, *Who cares?!* The men most likely.

But the women would secretly be glad that I don't have it

all together because I have it all together at work. There are no two-headed showers at work. I'm in charge.

I'm a bad ass, a force not to be reckoned with, an opponent worthy of respect. I made the cover of *Executive Elite* magazine last year. They paid a tribute to women executives. I think they figure if they throw a woman on the cover two times a year they can say they support our advancement. What I found obnoxious was the title: Don't Dismiss Her Because She's Blonde and Beautiful. Uh? Was this title chosen before or after you all had lobotomies? I felt like calling Sheryl and saying, *They really don't get it, do they?!* I know what she'd say.

My kids are solid. Adam, my first born, is majoring in accounting and will intern on Wall Street in May after he graduates, and Janie is double majoring in biology and Middle Eastern studies. She speaks Farsi. Yes, I have a beautiful, blonde daughter who speaks Farsi. But please ... don't *dismiss* her.

Perhaps I'm sensitive. Perhaps I'm feeling dismissible. I should have it figured out at home. Mike should want me more. I weigh eight pounds more than when we got married. Eight pounds! Not forty-eight. Eight. That's a sick comment, as if being thin is what makes someone loveable. Can I erase that comment? No? Then for the record, I apologize. I'm not sure how to express that I have it together. I really do ... he should want me. I cook, I plan incredible birthday get-aways. I earn obscene amounts of money, I have two beautiful, smart children. We do. I mean *we* have two beautiful, smart children. I serve on the boards of three non-profits and I'm almost done with my manuscript. I'm writing a book titled *The Disciplined Leader.*

Mike will often say to me, "You're the most amazing woman I know." It used to sound sincere. Sweet. The last few years it's had more of an edge. Not sure whether he's trying to appease me when I'm cranky, mock me when I coordinate schedules, or just fill up the silence that's now grown between us.

Amazing? Some days it's more believable than others. What I'm definitely not is perfect. And not being perfect terrifies me. My perfection terrifies my employees. They do not screw up. They know my risk tolerance is low. We have systems and processes and workflow design that were heralded in several case studies. Discipline has been a long time companion. Maybe that's what Mike sensed … discipline was my best friend, often a first choice. I'm guilty of saying family comes first and then not honoring that statement. Guilty.

My marriage has fallen apart so slowly I never stopped to fully absorb that the accumulation of disregard and disrespect would lead here, but how could it not? I sometimes wonder if this is the price I paid for my career, for my quest to have it all. All the worry, all the stress, the hard work, the exhaustion, the hours put in, the never being able to get out of the race for fear of losing all the effort already invested—for what? For a magazine cover? For a million dollar book deal? For a failed marriage? I tell myself that I created jobs, thousands of jobs, that I was a role model for other women, for my daughter, that I advanced dialogue about economic principles to ensure our country's economic future, but at what cost? I'm smart. Some how, some way, couldn't I have figured out how to really have it all?

But the truth is I don't have it all together and I've been too scared to sit down and say to my own husband that our marriage is broken. I fear I know what he'll say, what he'll do. I'm not sure why I think I should be perfect, or how these expectations got so high. When did I give these expectations so much of my power? I'm honestly not sure what I'm afraid of more; letting go or failing.

◂ ▾ ▸

Exploring Leaders' **Secrets**

Like Lyza, some of us prioritize our careers and companies, choosing the workaholic grind at the expense of distanced spouses, children, friends or the lack thereof. Some of us pursue a vision doggedly, only to successfully attain the vision and realize too late that it does not fulfill our now more mature, more evolved values, thus leaving us empty and disillusioned. Others of us use work as an excuse to not deal with the issues, disappointments or turmoil in our personal lives, preventing necessary growth that would enable us to lead even more effectively. Later in life, Lyza questions her pursuit of a career, a magazine cover, and perfection and wonders in hindsight if these aspirations were worthy of the cost.

The cost of pursuing success can exact an emotional, physical, mental or spiritual toll that may not ever be fully paid off until leaders consciously understand these costs and choose how to best invest in their own lives.

Lyza's unwillingness to face her marital problems, for fear of it truly failing—or for fear of having to admit that she failed—reflect her desire to prevent her mask of perfection from cracking.

Is it possible then, to realize a vision without sacrificing our own sense of self? Yes, but it requires letting go ... of a lot. Letting go of others' expectations, of others' values, letting go of our own unrealistic expectations, of the pursuit of perfectionism, of appearances of having it all together, letting go of the need to not be perceived as a quitter, of throwing good money after bad, or for thinking that letting go defines us as weak.

Exactly what we should be letting go of versus what we should be committing to is different for every one of us. What we all have in common are the definitive moments in the leadership journey when we must face a "letting go" decision that will reflect our true values and shape the course of our future path. Letting go can be one of the hardest things for leaders to do because it is often perceived as counterintuitive to the lessons we are taught about perseverance, resilience and determination. The idea of "letting go" becomes synonymous with failure, when in fact letting go can lead to greater success and peace.

Letting go is not always an observable action, sometimes it's the resolution of an inner struggle—it's a values based mind-set. By asking: *What is the current and future value of staying committed? What is the current and future value of letting go?* we are better able to discern the choices we need to make for aligning our internal belief systems and values with our external decisions.

Sometimes we hold onto something so tightly we squeeze the life and beauty right out of it, fooling ourselves into thinking that our unwavering commitment was a good choice. Sometimes we hold onto something carelessly, discarding it mentally, physically, spiritually or emotionally, and the cost of this energy leak goes on and on unnoticed until one day we realize we are depleted. We fool ourselves into thinking that our half-hearted commitment was healthy and whole. Commitment might be the fastest way to perpetuate failure and hurt, creating a lost opportunity to start over and work on something with a greater chance of fulfillment and success. Inversely, consciously re-committing may give us a chance to express other values without the regret of wondering if we gave up too soon.

The price leaders pay for leading can be quite high. The cost of masking our truth—hiding our imperfections, vulnerabilities and failures for fear of being perceived as unworthy of our leadership role or unworthy of our followers; or the cost of not facing our fears to avoid conscious, difficult decisions about how to move forward more successfully—can bankrupt a leader.

"Perfectionism becomes a badge of honor with you playing the part of the suffering hero."

–DR. DAVID D. BURNS, Psychologist, Author & Professor

• • •

"For which of you, intending to build a tower, sitteth not down first, and counteth the cost, whether he have sufficient to finish it?"

–LUKE 14:28, *King James Version*

CONCEPTS

- Loyalty

- Failure

- Commitment

- Work-life balance

- Inflection points in our lives for "do-overs"

- Means justifying the ends

- Cost of leadership

REFLECTING ON YOURS

1. What must you let go of to move forward?

2. Giving up and letting go are not the same ... where do you see the differences in your own choices?

3. Where in your life might you need a "do-over"?

4. Do the "means of your life" justify the outcomes in your life?

5. What has it cost you to lead?

"If I am not for myself, who will be?"

–PIRKE AVOTH

PAUL

ARCHITECT

BUILDIN' YOURSELF

JUDITH JUMPED DOWN my throat the other day. I was working from home. Big hospital deal. We get this one, we could get the whole system. I was wrong. I admit that now, but at the time I was focused—in the zone. Jarod, my son, flew into my office demanding dinosaur time. He knows the rules. He knows that when my doors are closed he is not to interrupt. My doors were closed. He was misbehaving and I lost it. But we have rules. Judith heard me yelling, came in, saw Jarod crying and I swear she has this look … I knew.

God, that look. It stops you in your tracks. Don't say it. I know. I *know*. Don't say it.

She said it. "Don't be her."

Please God, let it not be true. That's why I'm here, Doc.

I'm her. Not all of her. But I am her. Three thousand miles away, and yet, she lives here. I have her quick wit, her insight. I have her ability to draw, to see things. But I'm selfish and proud too. Some days I can get through the whole day without even thinking about her. Some days, like when I shave, the memories suck the wind out of me. Praise Jesus.

That's what I said in the early days. It's what I say now, but more of an inside joke. Can I back up a sec, Doc? Is that allowed? Okay.

At 22 I was made *Director of Marketing*. For three days I walked on cloud nine. Then … I called Mother.

"What's the title above you?" Those were her first words.

Manager.

"How long will it take to get that title?"

Typically, a year.

I got it in seven months … but I was too busy to call. And even busier when I got *Senior Manager*. It was tempting to call her when I made *VP*. But I knew better by then. No title would ever be quite enough.

Praise Jesus! I said that a lot. Mainly because I knew it drove her crazy. Mother went to Temple Bethel as a child. But

Father was a Methodist. When Father died in the crash she said she was done with Christians. I was six. Charles was two. Father was dead and we were eating bagels and hard-boiled eggs so fast that I thought Shiva was a cousin. I missed the jello molds and casseroles. What I'd give for a Methodist potluck. I grew angry. No—no gefilte fish! I want meringue!

Over the years, Mother would come home with announcements.

"Deborah and Marty had a baby boy."

I would call out, "Praise Jesus!"

That pissed her off, and so, over time, I got even better and more Baptist sounding when I said it. Praise Jesus!

"Ruth and Saul got Rachel into an exclusive Jewish Day Camp."

"Praise Jesus!" I yelled louder.

"Wouldn't you boys like to go?"

"When pigs fly out of Abraham's—sorry, Doc."

Mother wore a huge amethyst ring … I turned the other cheek. It's why the scar. Yes, she hit me. Her ring split my lip wide open. Praise Jesus.

She was done with Christians but not country clubs. There were no Randalls and Pinsons at the Belle Haven. More like Feldmans and Goldsteins. Parents full of Bloody Mary's and teenagers full of secrets. She took us swimming at the club every summer.

It's sort of like standing at the edge of the pool, Doc.

Look at me! Look at me!

Waiting for Mother's attention. Desperate for someone to cheer me on—for somebody to notice. To watch. To praise. Desperate for someone to make me matter.

Look at me! I'm about to dive! Look at me, Mother! I'm about to jump.

Look at me! Look at meeeeee!

Sorry, Doc.

And that's after you learned how to swim. Before, you were afraid. In fact, you might have been terrified. You didn't know how to keep your chin above water, let alone your eyeballs. That's when you need faith in yourself most of all—right before you jump.

I still remember my dad teaching me to swim. I was petrified watching him remove my floaties. He didn't give me a man-up speech. He didn't dismiss my feelings. I just remember him putting a hand on my shoulder, leaning down, and saying, "Paul, you got this. You may go under, you may drink a little water, but I guarantee in an hour, son, you'll be a shark."

He gave me faith. In me.

My brother Charles sat on the side of that pool for hours the summer he was five, just making up scenes in his head. He imagined them plucking him off the bottom of the deep end. Trying to resuscitate him. Shaking their heads in hopelessness. Mother pouring herself a drink. Swearing she never took her eyes off him. That poor kid was more exhausted imagining his drowning than we were from swimming all day.

It was painful to watch him. I knew he was scared. Mother helped as only she could, bribery, followed by, "Don't be a sissy. Your ancestors survived the Assyrians and Hitler." That worked wonders. All he wanted was for her to cheer him on, for her to have faith in him so he could have faith in himself.

I offered to be his buoy—offered to hold onto him all summer. He refused. At first I got it, but then you get angry you know? A little embarrassed that he wouldn't get on with it already.

He learned to swim his sophomore year in college. Kate. A cute girl took a shine to him one summer and he learned to swim overnight. That little **** I swear, one good kiss ... but he needed her. I get it. He wasn't moved by Mother's threats or my coddling. He was moved by someone's faith in his own ability. Is that wrong, Doc? Is it wrong to want just one person to believe in you?

I sound like a rebel. I wasn't. I memorized some of the Torah. I made Matzah balls. I had a Bar Mitzvah. I married a Jew. But it was never enough to get Mother to say, "You're a shark, son." In her eyes, I'm chum.

I believe that the cry "Look at me!" MUST be answered with—"I'm watching! You can do it! You can jump! Jump!"

Ever feel like you're standing at the side of the pool, Doc? Only nobody's watching? Nobody's saying you matter? Nobody has faith in you.

Praise Jesus! Ha!

My favorite first course—grilled shrimp ... wrapped in bacon. I praise all the *Junior Managers*, all the *Directors*. We celebrate every month. Big successes, and the mini ones. We throw a party with champagne, balloons, tons of food. Gluten free, vegetarian, low fat, organic—I do care about them. And they know it. They know they matter. Everybody jumps! I pay attention. Everybody jumps. Praise Jesus!

You know, Doc, I've spent my whole life praising Jesus for only two reasons—to piss off my mother, and to get closer to my dad, but I think underneath it all, I do it for me. I tell myself I matter. I am a Great White.

Last year I came across this saying:

May you be well.
May you be happy.
May you be free from suffering.

It's one of my favorite meditations.

May you be well.
May you be happy.
May you be free from suffering.

It's a loving kindness meditation. Buddhist.

May you be well.
May you be happy.
May you be free from suffering.

It's a good bridge between pecan pie and rugelach.

Exploring Leaders' **Secrets**

When the world doesn't support us, when it seems in fact, to turn its back on us, how do we keep faith in ourselves? As a child, an adult's word of encouragement is sometimes all we need to believe in our own abilities, but what if these words don't get said? What if someone tells us through actions or words that we don't matter? What if we, like Paul, do not hear words of affirmation? How then do we hear all the world's noisy feedback and learn to accept, love and believe in our own worth?

Leaders with low self-esteem or little confidence in themselves continually seek others' approval, sabotage their success or underachieve. Our search for significance undermines our personal power. When our power rests externally in others' praise or affirmation then our ability to persevere or to feel resilient relies on the words and actions of others and not our own.

Pleasing others or searching for signs of significance from others undermines the energy required for leading ourselves, let alone the energy required to lead others. And therein often lies a paradox.

We are told not to care about what others think of us, but then someone hugs us or provides us with positive feedback and we feel better about ourselves. Someone criticizes us and it hurts. Someone says, just with a look, that they do not care for the way we present ourselves or that they do not care for our choices, and we immediately feel judged.

Leaders must choose what to let in and absorb. As leaders we must choose who has the "right" to influence our sense of self. We cannot stop people from providing their opinions, but we can decide which opinions matter to us. As humans we develop a sense of self in part by our connection with others and their reflection back to us. The good news is that as we grow older we can refine our skills for more effectively integrating constructive feedback from those whose influence and connectivity we choose to let into our lives for healthy reasons and for those whose influence, or lack thereof, we need to block to prevent an unhealthy sense of self.

When leaders remember that their followers are little kids in adult bodies, seeking approval and affirmation, they can more effectively provide sincere, specific feedback and praise to their followers. While we cannot base our value of self by others' opinions, leaders are still encouraged to provide genuine feedback so as to inspire those they lead and help them develop their own sense of self worth.

We are born seeking connection. We cannot shut out the world, but we can learn to quiet the critics and to embrace the caring truth-tellers who pick us up and dust us off after battle, hug us, and gently tell us where we could have fought harder or performed better so that we can indeed do better, because we know we matter.

"I can be changed by what happens to me. But I refuse to be reduced by it."

—MAYA ANGELOU

• • •

"The privilege of a lifetime is being who you are."

—JOSEPH CAMPBELL

CONCEPTS

- Encouraging and supporting others to believe in their own worth
- Encouraging and supporting others to claim and act on their power
- Recognizing our individual significance
- Believing in and loving ourselves
- Claiming and retaining our power
- Defining our own worth

REFLECTING ON YOURS

1. Who are you trying to please?

2. How do you let others know that you believe in their worth?

3. When or to whom do you give your power away?

4. How might you start reclaiming your power?

5. Can a leader love and lead his/her followers without first loving and leading him/herself?

6. How do you know you matter?

◂▴▸

"If you don't like what's being said, change the conversation."

—DON DRAPER, *Mad Men*

LEILA

ACTIVIST

TAKIN' A STAND

DO YOU KNOW what BMW stands for in China?

Be. My. Wife.

You laugh. Chinese women want cars. Know what the Chinese government wants? Fuel.

What kind of car do you all drive? SUVs? Sports cars? The word Prius make you cringe? You're all addicts.

For decades what have we gotten? Lip service. "We will reduce our dependence on foreign oil." Reduce our dependence.

We live in an oil economy and we're more dependent than ever. We don't have an energy problem, we have an addiction problem. This company is addicted too.

No, please. Hear me out. I thank the Board for letting me speak tonight. I'm sincerely appreciative, so please let me use my ten minutes to share a different perspective. A perspective that could help this company for the better.

I was three when I lost my father to the Gulf War. You remember … it was also called the Persian Gulf War, First Gulf War, Gulf War One, Kuwait War, First Iraq War, but that was after "Iraq War" became identified instead with the 2003 Iraq War which we also refer to as "Operation Iraqi Freedom." Yeah.

Most people today just remember Desert Storm. For most people back then, it was the war … over there, about Iraq. About oil.

It's so stupid. It's not like we don't have answers. Natural gas, ethanol, methanol. We have the resources, we are reducing, we are fracking, but we don't really get it. We'll increase tax incentives for commuters who drive their gas sucking cars, while we simultaneously stick it to public transit users. Yep, it's true, not joking.

Do you leaders ever question if you're having the right conversation, with the right people, at the right time about the right stuff? Or are you so busy going through the motions you miss the most critical conversations of all—the ones that matter—the ones that create real change? I'm referring to our lovely political leaders, our business leaders, you—the Board, and me—all of us so called leaders who refuse to change the conversation. I'm talking about societal leadership … or do you just want to sit on your couch, watch the pundits, nod your glassy-eyed heads and complain about the price at the pump? No, I know, the price of fuel is down this week … everything must be right with the world.

Ten of the last eleven recessions were preceded by spikes in oil prices. You look surprised. It's. An. Addiction.

Like any addiction it destroys you. People only stop shooting up when their illusions crash in negative consequences. What are we waiting for? What does hitting rock bottom look like for America?

For addicts, it's a ruse. As long as they can fool you, it's all good; but when it starts to fracture, to fall apart, they slip from being a functioning addict to a person possessed by the fix.

America used to be a leader of nations. We used to function. Today? We're fifth in innovation, twenty-second in literacy, twenty-third in science, thirtieth in math. But the good news? We rank Number 1 in anxiety disorders.

I was 13, on the floor studying mitosis vs. meiosis, listening to my Walkman when I looked up at the TV. The towers were on fire. My oldest brother was in the World Trade Center when the first plane hit. Josh worked for Marsh, just a few floors below Cantor Fitzgerald. He made it out. Broken ankle. That's it. One of the lucky, everyone said. Except he can't hold a job. PTSD.

Our family avoided war after my dad died, we loathed it. But 9/11 ... Ben, my middle brother, wanted vengeance. He enlisted, and mom took me to anti-war protests like some mothers take their kids to soccer games.

The damage addiction causes ... we're living a double life.

While you're talking about recycling, global warming, composting and sleeping well at night knowing that your check just saved some rhino, soldiers die to fill your fuel tank, soldiers die to fuel our plant operations. A father gets killed. A brother almost goes up in flames. My brother Ben died in Kandahar trying to save his platoon. An ambush. No survivors. No heroes—just loss.

And before you judge me, I'm all for saving rhinos. God bless those people who want to save rhinos, but rhinos didn't kill my dad. Rhinos didn't kill my brother. Oil burned up their lives.

People don't understand addictions. "Just this once" becomes your life. You can't stop, even though you know it's completely trashing you. It's not an issue of how much oil, there's plenty of oil. We just can't afford it. And we're too stupid, too stoned to see it.

Last week I attended the memorial at Ground Zero. I told this guy that I almost lost one of my brothers in the attacks. He joked, "I hope he didn't survive just to be a part of the financial crisis." I didn't find it funny.

The '90s were all about technology. The 2000s e-commerce. And now? Now it's about resources. Clean energy. But the conversation is wrong—it's not about fracking. We're all so stupid we can't even change the conversation and get it right. We're all fracking morons. We must defund our addiction, we must defund evil. We must lead the way. Show the world that we can be a profitable company without oil.

No, no, I know my time is up. I'm done. Thank you. Sincerely, thank you for listening.

◄▼►

Exploring Leaders' **Secrets**

Leila's activism in a board meeting reveals the need for leaders to listen, be sincerely open and approachable, and accept feedback and input from those whom they may not immediately agree with on divisive issues. What happens when followers are courageous enough to challenge the thinking and behaviors of their leaders? A lot of positive change: industry, societal, economic, political and global change … to name a few.

When followers challenge leaders to change the conversation, to course correct for better policies and procedures, refine a vision for the betterment of many or avoid disastrous consequences, leaders may incorrectly assume that followers are standing *up* to them in opposition, when in fact, followers might be standing up *for* them and everyone's future success.

Leaders sometimes find it easier to surround themselves with sycophants (who doesn't like to hear positive remarks from their followers?!), however, when people avoid healthy dialogue and debate, or avoid contradicting the leader all together, the bigger, better, bolder ideas and solutions get lost, and then everyone loses.

Leaders must invite their followers to change the conversation, challenge the thinking, present new perspectives and participate in ideation as a natural course of business. Sharing diverse perspectives, participating in cross-functional associative thinking, and challenging the status quo lead to creative and potentially more profitable outcomes—profitable outcomes on multiple levels, not just economic.

Two-way communication is critical to a leader's success, especially when we lead in times of rapid-growth or significantly changing environments.

Leaders who provide clear, safe channels of communication for addressing cultural, operational, financial, strategic and other critical issues not only leverage more creative and innovative opportunities, they garner increased buy-in and loyalty from their followers.

What are followers asking for from their leaders? Relevancy.

Change is not easy, and moral and ethical changes are often the hardest shifts of all. But shifting or evolving your perspective is not a sign of weakness, nor is it about sacrificing your moral compass. Change is about adapting, expanding perspective and aligning behaviors that reflect a more evolved moral compass for a better future: civil rights, human rights, gender equity. When leaders candidly share their thoughts and insights behind a changing perspective they expand their followers' understanding, compassion and perspective. It is only when leaders flip-flop on their perspective, pandering to certain factions of their followers, that they lose credibility, integrity and are diminished in the eyes of many more followers than those who simply refuse to buy-into the new vision.

For leaders to stay ahead of an ever-evolving landscape, they must listen to the relevant, rising voices of their constituents—both inside and outside of their companies. By remaining flexible and open to new ideas, leaders better adapt to the wants and needs of their customers and shareholders, they capitalize on more innovative tools and strategies to maintain their competitive advantage, and they stay ahead of the curve.

"Always go too far, because that is where you will find the truth."

–ALBERT CAMUS

• • •

"In rough terrain, the rigid become irrelevant."

–MILTON PEDRAZA

CONCEPTS

- Speaking up and challenging the status-quo
- Honoring our moral convictions
- Staying relevant as a leader
- Taking a stand when it is neither safe nor popular but necessary to our moral code
- Being open to change
- Listening to our followers

REFLECTING ON YOURS

1. When was the last time you changed a conversation for the better?

2. When, where and how do you give voice to your personal moral code in the workplace?

3. How have you created safe channels for your followers to challenge the status-quo?

4. How do you initially respond to followers who challenge you to change?

5. How are you challenging yourself to stay relevant to and for your followers?

"Be so good
they can't
ignore you."

–STEVE MARTIN, Comedian,
Actor, Singer, Songwriter, Playwright

RONNIE

HIGH SCHOOL
FOOTBALL COACH

Seein' You

Press Conference

Reporter 1: You seem giddy, Coach Parker. How does it feel to have just led the Meerkats to a victorious state football championship?

Ronnie: Wow! Amazing! I want to thank God first and foremost. It's His victory. And our opponent, those Fire Ant boys—they played a great game. They were tough. I feel very blessed with my coaching staff and our players. True team effort.

Press Conference Coordinator: John, 4th row.

John–Reporter: This was a slow game. A huddle on almost every play. Why?

Ronnie: Gentlemen, a huddle is like going to church. The sermon—your game plan. You execute the plan all week, then you return to church for a reset—the next game plan. Our huddle is a mini game plan, a homily for what we need to execute on the field.

Coordinator: On the left, Peter.

Peter–Reporter: What's your coaching philosophy?

Ronnie: In football, the 11 men on the field are disciples—just like in the Bible. Well, minus Judas. But most people think of disciples as just followers. Just learners. It's more dynamic than that. They are *multipliers*. To be a disciple is to be called to make new disciples. It's not enough to be focused and disciplined, to play like a cohesive team with respect and trust. I tell my boys—once they know these things on the field, they know these things in life. Just like any good disciple of any good cause it's about helping others believe in what you're doing. Believing in your goal. Build your fan base. Build your followers.

Coordinator: Question in the back.

Stan–Reporter: What's the secret sauce of your success?

Ronnie: Secret? There's no secret. The sauce is "habits and beliefs." The key to winning on and off the field comes down to your habits and beliefs. If we instill the right habits, with the right beliefs—we win. Your life today is the product of your habits and beliefs.

How productive or lazy are you? Product of your habits and beliefs.

How happy or unhappy are you? Product of your habits and beliefs.

How successful or unsuccessful are you? Product of your habits and beliefs. Fellas, habits and beliefs form the person you are: your words—your actions.

Coordinator: Dave, second row.

Dave–Reporter: What's the "I see you" on the back of your cap? Got eyes on the back of your head?

Ronnie: Meerkats are from Southern Africa—the Kalahari Desert. The Bushmen who live in the remote wasteland of the Desert greet one another with "I see you. " It's their hello, but it's more than hello, it's—"I see your soul. I see your humanity. I see your dignity and I respect you." It's about understanding. When someone says "I see you," the Bushmen respond with, "I am here." You acknowledge that you have been seen and understood and that your personal dignity has been recognized.

To be seen and understood—there are few things valued more than these. My boys wear their Meerkat caps between classes, in the hallways, the lunchroom, school events, it reminds students to respect and understand one another. Multipliers these boys are—Multipliers!

Coordinator: Eric, far right.

Eric–Reporter: Thoughts about that interception right before the half?

Ronnie: It would have been a great pass … if No. 23 played for us.

John–Reporter: You were down by seven at the half—what happened in the locker room?

Ronnie: At half-time I asked my boys two questions. First, I asked 'em, "What jobs do we need done?" On the field, it's not about long-term strategy. It's about executing in your role—getting your job done. We had a clearly defined goal—winning the game—but to achieve the goal you have to play your role, you gotta hunker down and get the job done. We weren't getting the job done.

The second question I asked 'em, "Imagine you are in a sinking rowboat surrounded by sharks. How would you survive?" Well, whaddya think?

Easy. Stop imagining! They gotta control their thoughts—their limiting beliefs. The ship's not sinking, you're not surrounded by sharks—focus on what's real. Focus on your role—your job and performing it well. Habits and beliefs fellas.

Coordinator: Don.

Don–Reporter:

What's so mighty about Meerkats?

Ronnie: What are you trying to say? That there's nothing mighty about Meerkats?! I'd say we were pretty mighty today—considering we beat a great team. I have the highest respect for the Fire Ants. They played their hearts out. They wanted to win. Our boys wanted to win. In sports, we all want to be the victor. There are many strategies, many ways to win, but ultimately, true victory is being a champion.

Meerkats form strong bonds—tight knit groups. Each and every Meerkat has a critical role—no different on the field— each player has a critical role. The players respect these roles, and they see the value every team member contributes.

Meerkats dig multiple tunnels to confuse and out maneuver their predator. We need multiple plays in our playbook to confuse and out maneuver our opponent.

There is more to winning than just being more aggressive than your opponent. Meerkats have fears too, real and perceived. Meerkats are afraid of planes. They think it's a hawk. A plane flies overhead—and everyone runs for cover. But they quickly come out of hiding and get back to their job.

No different than humans, we have fears too. But we can't play in the fear. Like the Meerkat we need to recover quickly, come back out and focus on the job. But unlike the Meerkat, we can learn to separate the real from the perceived, the hawk from the plane. The better we are at facing our fears, separating the real fears from the stories in our head—the mightier we become—the stronger we are in our ability to lead ourselves, play well and win.

Coordinator: Eric.

Eric–Reporter: What should every high school football player take away from your victory today?

Ronnie: Focus on the goal. Habits and beliefs, fellas, if you don't love the practice—you're in the wrong game. And only when you're in the right game can you be a Multiplier.

◂ ▾ ▸

Exploring Leaders' **Secrets**

Most coaches and players dream of being champions. Not all coaches and players become champions. Coach Parker believes to be a true champion we must defeat our internal rivals as much as we defeat our external ones; fight for a cause or belief system larger than ourselves; support others in doing the same; manifest a personal definition of success for the good of ourselves and others; and accomplish the goal.

Sports are a prominent and prevailing part of human society. Coaches and players often serve as metaphors or models for leadership and team play. The list of sports analogies that apply to life is long: *do not be a bystander; keep your head in the game; keep your eye on the ball; don't get blind-sided; we're fourth and inches from our goal line*, etcetera. However, there is one sport-life comparison that is discussed less frequently—how the habits and beliefs of coaches and players define them as leaders.

In sports, as in life, there is a strong tie between our habits, beliefs and results. Coach Parker's conviction in his beliefs defines him and his coaching style. While winning is an obvious common goal, it's the less obvious goals on *how* they will play to win that create true champions. Ronnie's playbook of the habits that his beliefs require— *every day, every practice, every game*—influence his discussions, decisions and actions. It is the alignment

229

between his habits and beliefs, (personally manifested through coaching), that lead him and his players to victory, both on and off the field. Coach Parker has a playbook. All leaders need a playbook that clearly defines their beliefs and outlines the habits that will best support their beliefs.

When coaches demand good habits from their players, the discipline of these habits often carries over into the players' personal lives. Members of the Meerkat football team wore their hats for all other students in the high school to witness. The concept of "I see you" was shared both on the field and through the corridors of the school. As in most high schools, the football players are influencers, and Coach Parker teaches these young leaders how to use their influential positions to be Multipliers for belief in individual dignity, respect and understanding.

Coach Ronnie Parker believes in the popular phrase, "the end justifies the means" but with a slight twist: "only if the means to achieve a good and noble goal are also good and noble." Sadly, too many leaders use this phrase as an excuse to achieve a goal by any means possible, including sacrificing their core values. By sewing the words "I see you" into the backs of his players' caps, Coach Parker reminds his players, and all those who see the message, that when we accomplish our mission, when we win, only if we have aligned *what we believe* with *how we play* can we call ourselves champions.

"We are what we repeatedly do. Excellence, then, is not an act but a habit."

—ARISTOTLE

. . .

"People don't want more information. They are up to their eyeballs in information. They want faith—faith in you, your goals, your success, in the story you tell."

—ANNETTE SIMMONS

CONCEPTS

- Seeing others
- Being seen
- Defining what it means to be a champion
- Being a team player
- Work ethic
- Habits and beliefs
- Being a Multiplier

REFLECTING ON YOURS

1. How are your personal habits and beliefs working for you?

2. Are some habits and beliefs better than others for achieving success?

3. Do you "see" your followers? How do they know you see them?

4. Will your playbook make you a champion?

5. How are you a Multiplier?

Bonus Chapter

Sneak peek from the upcoming new book by

AmyK Hutchens

The
Secrets
Women Keep

For More Resources and Information, Visit:

www.AmyK.com

"When you believe in yourself more than you believe in food, you will stop using food as if it were your only chance at not falling apart."

— GENEEN ROTH

LEAH

AEROSPACE ENGINEER
AGE 37

MUNCHIN' SOME LOVIN'

I AM AT WAR with what's on the plate in front of me. I'm defending a full frontal assault, the dispute in my head more contentious than any political debate. Do I or don't I inhale?! It's a serious question. There's a slice of coconut cake assembled before me. The cake itself is textured with air pockets and nibs of coconut shavings that shimmer in the chandelier's light above me. Do I sound like I'm a 7 year old at Disney World, ogling Cinderella's Castle? I might as well be: it's that same pathetic, drooling state of pure joy. Don't judge. You have a secret lust like this too. And don't pretend it's for something more elegant, like a '79 Bordeaux. It's got cheese in it, and you know it.

This cake has exactly four layers. Incredible, but true. Four. Each layer is separated from the one below by a thin yellow line of lemon curd. And separated from my hips by a thin line of self-control. Very thin. The *line,* not the hips. The cake's slope from peak to plate has created an avalanche of crumbs that now reside in a smear of cream cheese frosting and lemon curd pooled on the large plate in which it rests, and that my finger now itches to swipe. If only I could swipe left and delete the whole slice. But alas, there's only one way to make it disappear.

Did we humans ever stand a chance? Humans have had an adversarial relationship with food from the beginning. Eve couldn't resist the temptation of an apple—or a peach if you prefer. I can understand the temptation of a peach. I've consumed more than one large bowl of peach cobbler on a particularly sad weekend. I picture Eve, before the Fall, blind naked, in the mood for a snack, feeling pretty bodacious and not caring at all about her body because she can't see her cellulite yet. But the moment her eyes opened, the moment she saw Adam checking her out, she suddenly felt the need to cover herself in some frumpy, green-colored fig leaves. One of her first thoughts had to have been, *Do these leaves make me look fat?*

For me, coconut cake is a bigger foe than chocolate or my

boss. My boss is impossible most days, perhaps even a tad infuriating, but overall, he's benign. Chuck continuously has these sudden changes in his "grand" vision. I'll pull everyone together, design a well thought-through operational plan, we'll start to execute it—and on a whim, he switches direction, demanding that we design a new plan … due yesterday. When I really think about all the times he's pulled this kind of stunt it's maddening. But harmless enough. He's just a classic visionary who's clue-free on the myriad of details it takes to make our clients really happy. Yet still, it makes me crazy. I know, I know: #FirstWorldProblems.

A day, thanks to Chuck, spent re-drafting plans that were magnificent to begin with, obliterates most of my will-power—but it's nothing compared to this coconut cake. If I even sample one taste of this gorgeous combination of vanilla and sugar mixed with a hint of the tropics, I will end up licking the plate. And not in a sexy way.

Food is comfort. This is not a news flash. I stuff down food to stuff down emotions. I know I am not alone in this endeavor. I googled *emotional eating* the other night right after I crunched down on my last nacho. In my defense, I ordered a skinny margarita. I clicked on an article containing a survey that asked me to select the three most common emotional reasons I eat from a list including: anger, anxiety, boredom, depression, dissatisfaction with my life, emptiness, fear, filling a void, loneliness, out of control, purposelessness, resentment, sadness, shame, and feeling unfulfilled.

Um … How 'bout, "Yes?"

I mean really, "select three?" All I get is three? I kept selecting buttons, and every time I chose a new one it deselected a prior one. Where is "All of the Above?" How could this survey not be designed with an "All of the Above" option?! *I need that option!* Yep, that was my actual thought! Add *embarrassment* to the emotional survey list. And pass the guacamole.

Food has always been a huge part of my life. I'm not Italian, nor Greek, nor from any stereotypical heritage that makes you say, *Well, of course!* But I was nursed from the bosom of a bountiful table nonetheless. One of my earliest memories is of homemade biscuits. Dense flour baked to a golden brown, smeared with cold, creamy butter and topped with tart homemade blackberry jam. A trifecta of parental love. My mother would rise extra early on Sundays, bake two dozen biscuits, fry bacon, scramble eggs and we would wake to the smell of security sautéed in heart disease. School days we were left to cold cereal and milk that often needed to be sniffed before it could be poured, but Sundays were a day where everything was grand. Big breakfasts, bold sermons and an entire afternoon of play-filled freedom before my dad would fire up the grill.

The wafting smell of lighter fluid and briquettes would find us four backyards away, and we would know that in less than twenty minutes my father would ring the huge cowbell he and my mother bought when they were dating. That cowbell summoned seventeen children from throughout the neighborhood, ages four to thirteen, to our backyard. You had to, "Churn to Earn." That was my dad's motto. Every kid in the neighborhood had to crank the large silver handle on our old-fashioned ice cream maker for three minutes if they wanted a bowl of real vanilla ice-cream on a warm Sunday summer night. No one complained. Optimists might even churn for four minutes, hoping for seconds.

I memorialize seasons first by food, then by activity. Summers are corn on the cob, cucumber salad, hamburgers, baked potatoes, ice cream and mini-crushes on boys. Lots of boys. Boys who started with pulling my pony-tails, then challenging me to bike wheelies, eventually leading to awkward, tentative kisses followed by clumsy attempts to unhook a bra strap. Fall is mulled cider, pumpkin pie, apple sauce and the anxiety of going back to school. New teachers, harder courses, rocky friendships and cliques, and night after night of homework when it grew dark before dinner. Family activities revolved around meals … the planning of, the shopping for, the preparation of, the setting of the table with seasonal decorations.

Winter is the classic Thanksgiving dinner through Christmas lamb all the way up to molten lava cakes for Valentine's Day, but molten lava cake wasn't popular until my twenties. As a kid, my mom and I made "All But the Kitchen Sink" brownies that contained both dark and white chocolate chips, walnuts, broken toffee pieces, oatmeal and coconut. Always coconut.

I'm a sucker for coconut. My kids start to fight in the backseat and I'll ask them to hand me a coconut protein bar. I tell myself it's good for me—a healthy choice. But how can a bar called *Chocolate Coconut Almond Brownie* with 22g of sugar, 4g of protein and 27g of carbs in its subdued, sophisticated packaging not be anything other than a grown up candy bar? And unfortunately, a very delicious one. I discovered them a few months ago when our company hired a Wellness consultant and she came in and replaced all of the chips, cookies and crackers in our cafeteria's vending machine with trail mix and protein bars.

I was having a particularly rough day. Bill, a fellow engineer who pisses on my ideas constantly, had run roughshod over my I.T. integration flow chart of a new interface we're going to use. It wasn't that his questions weren't valid, it's just that after every time he asked me an insulting question, he then praised Marsha, our Account Representative. Marsha's curves, unlike mine, are in all the right places. She's kid-less with an endless supply of big, beautiful, white teeth. Mine are fifty shades of off-white, but I'm investing in my children's teeth at the moment. That afternoon found me a little teary-eyed, until I discovered that not every snack in the machine tasted of sawdust. One of them, the *Chocolate Coconut Almond Brownie* bar, tasted like affection.

I can deal with Bill's criticism of me and his preference for the young filly, Miss White Strips. My problem is that I start to wonder why I'm always left out when it comes to receiving affection. If affection is going to be directed at anyone, what does it say about me if I'm always left out? And I am left out—

but mainly by me. Sometimes I wonder if the affection that I'm craving most is from myself. I can be a bit brutal, especially when I pass by a mirror, step into a dressing room, or stand next to some wench, I mean waif, dressed in spandex.

Math is my forte. I've always been good at math, and there is one very special equation I've understood since I was four years old. Food equals love. I'll churn the ice-cream crank for a full hour just to hang out with friends and family. And possibly get a triple scoop. Am I alone in the understanding of this equation? Don't kid yourself. Food is rarely about hunger. Sure, I can get famished as much as the next person, but that's unusual. The more common scenario is that I'm eating to console, soothe, buoy, celebrate or to fill some hunger that cannot be named from among the four food groups.

I'm not sure when I swapped biological hunger for emotional hunger. It might have been the summer I was thirteen and all of the sudden every boy in camp noticed that I was sporting a bra I very much needed. The unwanted and unexpected attention was surprising, disarming and overwhelming. I remember only too well that the easiest way to hide double Ds was to grab an extra serving, of um, anything and put my head down and eat slowly. To this day when I am uncomfortable, not sure of my next move or know the best words to use around men, I find it best to fill my mouth with food. It's much better than filling my mouth with my *foot*.

Thirteen was also the summer I started my period and discovered I have an incredible talent for crazy-combo cravings.

A lot of women don't like it when we talk about being pre-period. Oh sure, they like the convenient excuse of PMS to avoid exercise and sex and to attract sympathy and support of a second helping of mashed potatoes. But, they're simultaneously concerned that if we admit our hormones are more volatile on some days than others then somehow we will be deemed as less in control than everybody else.

But let's be candid—when the thought of caramel-fudge ice-cream, potato chips, pickles, sauerkraut and consuming an entire cow elbows out all other thoughts, I know I am 48 hours away from starting my period. Yep, it's that straightforward. And woe to the food that is set in front of me during these 48 hours because it will disappear faster than you can say *chocolate covered potato chips.*

The problem with food is that we cannot walk away. Alcoholics can abstain from liquor, but stopping eating is never a cure for anything. Sex addicts can go into therapy, but … they … can … sorry, lost my train of thought.

And yes, I can do the whole *rabbit* package and snack on baby carrots and bark, but after a few days of lean chicken and lemon broccoli my body cries out for real food. I'm like a wild child who starts throwing mini temper-tantrums until I'm offered something soothing, something comforting, something that says *I hear you and love you,* something positive from my family … or at least something from the carbohydrate family. I'm craving affection.

My husband is amazing in some ways. He loves me unconditionally, but he will not have a conversation with me about anything serious until after I eat pasta. It's a joke, but not really. The worst fight we ever had was when I was coming off a six day, pepper-soup fast. Dan swore if he ever tried talking to me about anything serious without post pasta serotonin running through my blood, to just go ahead and shoot him. "Less painful," he said. I find it endearing that he gets me, but it's also annoying that it's true. I shouldn't need pasta to talk finances with my husband, but then my friend Mindy says she can't talk finances with her husband without vodka, so maybe pasta is better. Or, maybe best of all: pasta with a good vodka cream sauce! Might this tasty combo make it easier for him to talk to me?

In a world that reveres tight, ripe rear-ends and worships whittled waistlines, I have a very big badunkadunk, and a waistline that is vexingly convex. Only when I cinch it with a huge belt can you separate my breasts from my belly button. Dan tells me I'm exaggerating—that he adores me for all my Rubenesque womanliness, but what I wouldn't give to look like Ms. Klum, just once, instead of Aunt Bee. And my thighs, goodness, how they thunder! I am woman … hear my thighs roar! I was only eleven when my PE teacher suggested that I might try wearing longer shorts. I've never forgotten this helpful suggestion.

Apparently, I'm not the only one who received these types of suggestions growing up. I have girlfriends in all shapes and sizes, and the two things we have in common, despite our dimensions, is our need for control and our need to self-criticize. And honestly, most of life is simply out of control and out of <u>our</u> control. And, we criticize ourselves before others do to lessen the sting. *This dessert I brought? It's leaning and lopsided.* But I said it first! And the crazy thing is, my BFFs wouldn't say it. Or they might, but in a supportive, none-of-us-are-perfect, I've-got-your-back way, so the only person stinging me—is me.

When things go smoothly, I tend not to eat or even think about eating, but darn it, when my computer got one of those nasty viruses last week, because someone in marketing stupidly clicked on a link that they thought was legit, I was sliding dollars into the cafeteria's vending machine so fast you would have thought I was in Vegas. I have felt out of control most of my life. I couldn't control my boobs bursting at thirteen, or stop the attention or derogatory remarks, or get the thin girls to appreciate my sense of humor, or the boys to appreciate my brain, or the magazines to stop awarding the covers to poster-children for androgynous heroin-addiction. The irony is that I can control what I put in my pie-hole and most days I choose, well … pie.

When do I replace pie with real sweetness? Real affection? I went to a seminar last night and heard a message that has given me new food for thought today. The speaker, a guru psychologist on weight loss, said, "The relationship we have with food directly reflects the relationship we have with ourselves." The minute he said it, something in my heart expanded, I started to feel a little teary, and I kicked myself for not grabbing one more piece of spanakopita before I sat down. Then he continued, and my thoughts of hors d'oeuvres bared themselves in the floodlight of his comment.

"Every woman's diet reveals how she sees herself and her place in this world," he shared. "Show me a woman living on celery sticks and I will show you a woman starving herself of love, warmth, comforting relationships and intimate, sloppy sex. Find me a woman with healthy hips, a bit of blueberry scone stuck to her upper lip, and a smile on her face, and I will show you the most empathetic listener and hard hugger. She's the one you always call when your life is imploding. Show me the woman who judges other women harshly and I'll show you the woman who is harshest with herself right before she eats a sleeve of cookies."

I identified. The coconut cake I mentioned earlier? It's still here. It's still taunting me, but it's a little less tempting now. I was just about to surrender to its exquisite beauty when a thought struck me. *What if I have been wrong all these years? What if the truth is that food does not equal love, but how we consume it does equal self-love?* Then perhaps, after all these years … I am still figuring out how to love myself. And it's this thought, in this moment, which makes me feel a little more full.

◄ ▼ ►

Vegetables are a must on a diet.
I suggest carrot cake, zucchini
bread, and pumpkin pie.

–JIM DAVIS

. . .

I don't stop eating when I'm full.
The meal isn't over when I'm full.
It's over when I hate myself.

–LOUIS C. K.

CONCEPTS

- Emotional eating
- Outlets for relieving stress
- Food as reflection of self-love
- Coping mechanisms
- Self-compassion and acceptance

QUESTIONS

1. Have you ever eaten when you're not hungry? If so, what hunger were you feeding?

2. How is the food you eat and the way you consume it a reflection of your relationship with yourself?

3. How do you celebrate and/or reward yourself personally and professionally?

4. What are 2 examples of your healthy and unhealthy coping mechanisms?

5. How do you offer yourself compassionate and unconditional acceptance?

6. How do you know that your love of self is healthy and whole?

amyk

SPEAKER.
THINK TANK FACILITATOR.
BUSINESS STRATEGIST.

AmyK focuses exclusively on the critical thinking skills and behaviors required for your brilliant leadership, innovation and self-actualization.

AmyK's CONFERENCE KEYNOTE TOPICS INCLUDE:

- IGNITE BRILLIANCE in your leadership
- IGNITE BRILLIANCE in your creativity & innovation
- IGNITE BRILLIANCE in your sales
- IGNITE BRILLIANCE in your communication
- IGNITE BRILLIANCE in your culture
- IGNITE BRILLIANCE in your story

"AmyK is a one-of-a-kind speaker!

It was an eye-opening experience to learn how all of us can tap into more creative and innovative thinking and behaviors."

-Rhett Asher, VP, Asset Protection, Data Security & Crisis Management, Food Marketing Institute

Want AmyK to speak or facilitate?

www.amyk.com
760.652.4030
contactus@amyk.com

Excellent! Warning: fasten your seatbelt!

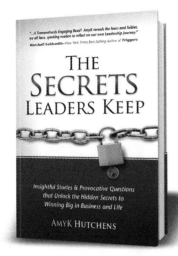